Advance praise for *Crimson Cowboy*:

"One of the most authentic books I have read. Sherman does a great job of bringing the reader fully into the world he knew as a high school, college, and NFL star. I couldn't stop reading it. Through the pages of *Crimson Cowboy*, you will literally experience the highs and lows of the incredible life journey of Sherman Williams."

—Dabo Swinney
CLEMSON UNIVERSITY HEAD COACH

"After years of crossing the line into criminal delinquency, Sherman Williams landed in Federal prison. His story is a vivid deterrent to anyone facing similar temptations. Passes to 'Get out of Jail Free' are in Monopoly—not real life."

—Craig Sager
TURNER SPORTS

"Sherman Williams has been to the top of the mountain as a football player, playing in a Super Bowl and a collegiate national championship game. He also experienced rock bottom off the field. The former University of Alabama and Dallas Cowboys standout has a story to tell that is cautionary and uplifting. It is definitely worth a read."

—Tommy Deas
EXECUTIVE SPORTS EDITOR
The Tuscaloosa News

"Sherman Williams was blessed with outstanding athletic ability, and a mother who supported him 100%. Greed can get the best of you when money becomes the most important thing in your life. Life is made up of choices, and Sherman made some bad ones. He did some things that even shocked me. His reason for writing this book is to try to keep others from making the mistakes he made. I appreciate his honesty in trying to help someone who may face the same temptations."

—Gene Stallings
HEAD COACH, Ret.
University of Alabama

CRIMSON COWBOY

CRIMSON COWBOY

Sherman Williams

Palmer Williams Group Media
Mobile, Alabama

DEDICATION

For my mother

This book is dedicated to a woman who was all a child could ask for in a parent. My mother was the type of person who never met a stranger. She had an infectious personality—one I took for granted more often than I realized the true beauty in her character. A hard working, sincere, and genuine woman, she would invite an entire high school football team over to spend the night at her house, not allowing anyone to leave until their stomachs were full.

Ms. Betty Ruth Williams

I love and miss you.

FOREWORD

You know the saying—you'll find what you're seeking in the most unexpected places. It's true, and one such place is Prichard, Alabama. Yes, it's small—about 22,000 residents, not very far from Mobile, and the average annual income hovers at poverty level. Jobs are scarce, drugs and property crime pollute the community, and education is a distant second priority—day-to-day survival is the first.

Prichard is a typical, southern, African-American town where hope flourishes, yet poverty reigns supreme. Citizens work hard, send their sons and daughters to defend our country, and they strive to save money so their children can go to college. The odds of success are formidable, but occasionally a young person beats those odds by achieving personal recognition on the national stage.

Sherman Williams beat the odds.

Stellar athletic prowess catapulted him to success in high school, college, and professional sports and, as a teenager, he avoided disaster by leveraging his God-given athletic ability—in fact, it was his commitment to education and athletics that aided in his avoiding negative distractions. He earned a full-ride scholarship to the University of Alabama, and it was there he reached his goals of being a star student and a star athlete.

By his junior year with the Crimson Tide, Sherman faced a critical decision—to stay in school, or take a chance with the NFL draft. The decision was his, but after consulting with his coach and family, Sherman decided staying in school would be of greater benefit. His decision paid off when the Dallas Cowboys drafted him in 1995. But, by the end of 1998, his meteoric rise to success was shattered when the Cowboys decided to cut him. He tried returning for a brief stint, but it didn't work out.

Life changed for Sherman—his arrest for operating a Texas-to-Alabama drug racket landed him in Federal prison for a fifteen-year sentence, and any hope he had of returning to the athletic limelight trickled to nonexistent. For some of us, consequences are nothing more than a bump in the road—for others, they are head-on collisions. The former is an inconvenience, a few minutes of lost time—for Sherman, the consequence held life-long implications.

So. As you read this book, take time to read between the lines because you probably know someone who is facing a difficult, life-changing decision—if so, refer them to the *Crimson Cowboy*. I'm certain anyone who reads Sherman's story will find it educational and inspirational. You see, it's all about listening to our voices followed by our moral compass. Sherman's love of God, his desire to succeed, and his will to teach others punctuates his personal lesson.

Allow his life to touch yours.

—A Friend

CHAPTER 1
The Dream

I wait on the bus as thousands of football fans snake their ways from the parking lot to the box office—scalpers hoping to get lucky, as well as fans who didn't buy a ticket the second they went on sale. Some of my teammates engage in conversations about people they saw tailgating—drunk men and beautiful women—others discuss the game plan. Since we're required to stay in our seats until we reach the area near the locker room, I gaze out the window, taking in everything as I listen to my music through earphones. Tupac and Biggie. I'm not sure why, but I seem to need music to diffuse the chaos around me that occurs before a game.

The bus inches through the crowd, and a middle-aged white man catches my eye. He is holding a sign that reads, "Go Cowboys—Kick Butt!" and, as I look closer, I notice he is wearing a white #20 Cowboys white jersey. Since jersey #20 wasn't retired yet, I think about how that jersey represents a number of great Cowboy players who wore it—players such as Ron Springs or Mel Renfro—and, here I am at the Super Bowl, about to pull on the same #20 jersey in my rookie year! I can't help thinking I might not deserve such an honor because I saw limited action during the regular season.

As the bus continues to creep forward, it seems as if the kick butt sign grew larger, as well as the #20 on his jersey. In fact, at one point, it literally consumes every inch of my being, and there is nothing else on my mind. He follows our bus, chanting, "Go, Cowboys, go Cowboys!" pumping his fist with his right hand and holding the sign in his left. This continues until the bus enters the part of the stadium where unauthorized people aren't allowed. As I watch from the window, the man slowly disappears into the crowd.

The team bus always segregates by function, with all offensive players on one bus followed by the defensive players on another. The special team players such as punters, field goal kickers, and the long snapper are free to choose which bus they want to ride. Every player has a seat with a window view, although there aren't any assigned seats. Still, there is an unwritten rule to ride to the game in my normal section, if not the same seat for every game. In any football season, people come and go—some are lost to injury, while others are released from the team. In this way, their replacements may or may not take the exact same seat as their predecessor, so there may be a slight rotation as the season goes by.

A stark reminder of how quickly things change in the NFL.

As we roll to a stop, we gather our belongings before exiting the bus. We wait for the cue to begin our exodus to the locker room—single file, one by one, neatly dressed in sport coats and ties. We step down into a small crowd of people consisting of stadium security, members of the press, and a limited, yet privileged, handful of fans.

Stadium employees stand by to grab our bags and escort us to the locker room while a handful of my teammates handle quick interviews with the media. A reporter from the Dallas Morning News approaches me, and I prepare myself for a few questions.

"How do you feel about making it to the Super Bowl as a rookie?"

"It's such an honor and privilege to not only play for the Dallas Cowboys organization, but to be drafted to play in the NFL. To make it to the Super Bowl is just the icing on the cake."

As I speak, I hear a fan in the background, yelling "Go, Cowboys! Go, Cowboys!" When the interview is over, I walk away from the reporter and, again, I notice a fan in a #20 jersey. It may be the same guy I saw on the bus, but he was too far away to tell. A barrier between us and the fans provide separation for security purposes—sometimes, the rush of a well-intentioned game-day crowd accidentally injures players.

A young Hispanic kids waits for me—he has my bags, and it's his job to escort me to the locker room. "Follow me, Mr. Williams," he orders, and we proceed down the corridor.

Foot traffic is everywhere as if everyone is on a mission. And, although it seems to be a typical pregame ordeal, it also feels hyped up because of the magnitude of the Super Bowl. The game is played at a neutral site, so most of the stadium employees are a bit indifferent because they could care less about who wins or loses. Some wish us luck, but most pass by without acknowledgment. I confess, I am relieved when we reach the locker room.

Once I join my teammates, it's easy to find my spot—all I have to do is follow the numbers on the lockers. But, the locker room is arranged differently than the seating on the bus—the offense and defense are mixed together by jersey number. So, my #20 is flanked by #19 on my right, and #21 on my left. John Jet (#19) is a punter and all-pro running back, and Dion Sanders is #21. Next to Dion is the all-time leading rusher of the NFL, #22, Emmit Smith, and next to him is the Super Bowl MVP cornerback, #24, Larry Brown.

I am so overwhelmed by the moment that I nearly forget the young Hispanic kid who is with me. He finishes placing my bags inside of my locker, and he is waiting. I reach into my wallet and give him a twenty-dollar tip—the tip is one of my personal signatures because it reflects my jersey number. I'm not certain if I am the only Cowboy or NFL player that has such a distinction—in retrospect, I'm glad my jersey number isn't #99!

In a way, Arizona reminds me of Texas because of its large Hispanic population. Many of the workers at the stadium are Hispanic, and that is a major difference from my home state of Alabama—in Alabama, people are Caucasian or African American. I consider it my great fortune to have the opportunity to travel and experience different cities, cultures, foods, and ethnic groups living in the U.S.

After the boy leaves, I inspect my gear starting with the most important item first—my cleats (cleats are still important today because Sun Devil Stadium has a natural grass surface.) Normally, I play in a Tiempo-style cleat that matches well with the natural-grass surface, but I make sure I have four or five types of cleats just in case the Tiempos aren't right. Typically, the equipment guys know which cleats work best for the surfaces we play on—but, as a player, I couldn't be sure until I actually wear the cleats on the specific surface. It's one of the primary reasons we have a walk-through on the game field the night before the game.

After choosing my cleats, I move all the other shoes aside to focus on checking my pads—the main task is to make sure I have everything I need. I sort through the equipment in my locker, and identify my shoulder pads, two thigh pads, two hip pads, helmet, and mouthpiece. So far, so good!

Next, my uniform. I pull it out of the locker, piece by piece, and I start putting it together starting with two pairs of socks—one pair on the inside for support, and the second which is the outer part of the official NFL uniform. It's ingrained in my mind that any deviation from the official NFL uniform is, potentially subject to a $5,000 fine.

My pregame ritual continues as I check my pants for any holes, tears, or improper alterations. Then I make sure the size is correct before moving on to the final and prized piece of any NFL player's uniform—my jersey. It isn't only a part of the uniform—it's part of my identity. And, as I pull it out of the locker, there is no way I can overlook the #20. For me, it is clearly the centerpiece of the all-white jersey. My number consists of a beautiful blue '2' and 'o', accented by three blue stripes on the sleeves.

After a detailed inspection, I lay it on the floor as if I were spreading it over a body. Then, I position the pants under it, as if the jersey has legs. I follow with my socks and shoes, and it appears as if a fully dressed human is lying on the floor in front of my locker.

I take a moment to picture myself wearing it.

There is business to attend to—I search my locker for a copy of the day's itinerary. It is twelve o'clock, and the itinerary indicates a 5:18 P.M. kickoff. I have a choice of taking the early bus which arrives five hours before kickoff, or the late bus which gets to the stadium an hour later. I choose the early bus so I will have plenty of time to get in a groove. I use the extra hours to relax and take it easy before the game without having to rush.

The itinerary indicates the first group of players will take the field at 3:00 P.M., which is two hours before kickoff—kickers, punters, and other members of the special teams. The second group will take the field ten minutes later—backs, tight ends, receivers, cornerbacks, safeties, and linebackers. The third group includes linemen and other players who weren't yet on the field—by 3:30 P.M., the entire team will be in place, ready to participate in warm-ups and stretching drills.

I dress in a warm-up suit and slippers—it's time to relax, and drift from locker to locker engaging in small talk with my teammates. Everyone tries to lighten the mood by discussing things such as playlists or current affairs—things not relevant to the game. Eventually, I return to my locker, plug my earphones in the CD player, and review the game plan. It's time to focus, and crank myself up for the game.

I envision myself in every play, choreographing every move in my mind. Dives. Sprint left. Jukes. I envision spins, and my signature 'shake' moves. I let them play in my mind, and when I open my eyes, I notice my teammates in their respective zones, preparing for their jobs in their own ways. Solitude is an unwritten rule in the locker room, and if a player is in his own zone, no one bothers him—it's a sign of respect. However, there's quite a bit of traffic in the locker room—some of my teammates nervously move back and forth, some going to or coming back from the showers. Some navigate through the crowd to reach the training room where they will be taped, wrapped, and treated by the training staff.

I decide to make my way to the trainer to complete my pregame check-up—I take any recommended or needed medication, as well report any ailments. Fortunately, everything checks out and I return to my locker to seek my own solitude. I slip on my earphones, and take a one-hour nap from one o'clock to two o'clock.

Then, a shower. I dress in my warm-ups again, and focus my mind on the game, visualizing myself running plays while cranking up the volume on my Walkman until it's time to return to the training room to get my ankles taped. Thankfully, I don't need to be fitted with knee or ankles braces! Looking around the locker room reminds me of how much of a toll football takes on the body. The tape winds tightly around my feet—uncomfortable and potentially dangerous if it cuts off circulation. So, I walk around the locker room without my shoes to give the tape a chance to stretch and loosen up.

Next, I put on both pairs of socks, slide on my slippers, and check with the coaches to see if there are any last minutes adjustments or changes to the plans, plays, or game signals. The coaches' locker room is located in a separate area from the players, but we have free access to them at any time. I talk to the offense and special teams coaches, and everything is a go—in fact, things are going so well, it seems as if I am in a dream.

I make my way back to my locker, and I notice Deion Sanders in his meditation mode, preparing to dress. He's a very spiritual guy—he believes in God, and he reads scriptures before all games. I ask him what verse he chose for the day—Psalm 23. As I approach him, he blurts out, "The Lord is my Shepard . . ."

"Amen, Brother," I affirm as we greet each other with a handshake.

Finally. Time to dress . . .

I put on my uniform piece by piece, starting with my fully padded pants. Before I can pull my shoulder pads over my head, I have to put on my cleats, and then it's back to the trainer's table to be spatted (additional tape applied over my shoes to provide additional ankle support. The tape resembles old-time spats . . .) Next are my shoulder pads and jersey, all as one—it's much easier to stretch the jersey over the pads first because it's designed to be a tight fit.

The only item left to complete my game-day uniform is my helmet. It's 'game day ready,' and I carefully examine it not for damage, but for the art. It is silver-gray with a blue and white stripe down the middle. It's most appealing feature is the blue five-pointed star located on each side. The Dallas Cowboy's insignia is one of the most recognized images in America, and anyone who sees it immediately associates it with the NFL organization. It's the trademark of the only a professional sports franchise known as 'America's team.'

I fall into a trance admiring the beauty of the helmet, but I jerk back to reality by the sound of Coach Switzer's voice yelling it's time for the first group to take the field— the signal for everyone in the first group to exit the locker room, including me, since I am a kick returner.

It's two hours before kickoff, and counting down. We enter the stadium, and small groups of fans are already in their seats. Media personnel lace the sidelines, bands rehearse, and marketing/promo people are busy doing what they do best.

Now, players are off limits.

The field is sectioned off to accommodate both teams, and players from each are in their designated areas. As I warm up, songs play in my head—rhythms groove as I move through my routine. Punters are punting, and kickers are kicking under the shining Arizona sun on a nice, warm day in January. A light breeze swoops down on the field as I line up to field my first punt—the kick leaves the punter's foot in a clean spiral, and it is a type of kick I track easily. I lock onto the punt, and I notice a slight drift as I track it—I follow the drift as the wind swirls within the stadium. Within seconds, it drifts over my head! I try to tap it down, but I run out of real estate, the ball sailing into the opposing team's warm-up area. It hits the ground, bouncing up into the pregame crowd on the sidelines.

That's cool, I thought as one of our ball boys chases down and retrieves the errant ball. *It's one of the reasons we go through the drills before kickoff—we don't want these things to happen during the game.*

I get back in line to return a few punts, then switch over to return a few kickoffs prior to our second group taking the field. After the second group arrives, we break off into groups with our position coaches to execute different drills. Once the third group comes out, we come together as a team to go through our stretch routine. After that, the offense and defense run through a prescribed set of plays. When we exhaust our warm-ups and drills, it's back to the locker room. We are on the field for about an hour and a half, and kickoff is only thirty-five minutes away.

The locker room has a different feel than it did a few hours ago—it's buzzing with players, coaches, trainers, and members of the media.

The game is imminent.

I'm ready—loose and relaxed. The smell of the freshly cut grass is in the air, tracked into the room on everyone's cleats. My adrenaline is flowing, my blood pumping, and I am sweating profusely—I am in game mode. Coach Switzer gathers us together, and we huddle in the center of the locker room—some standing, some kneeling on one knee as Coach begins his pregame speech.

"Gentlemen, this is what you worked toward for your entire life—to be in a situation like this. Take advantage of the opportunity. Make every second count."

He's right.

As a young boy, playing in the back yard at my mother's house, I imagined the bright lights, and the crowd yelling and screaming my name. Now, here I am, a grown man in a dream-come-true situation. As Coach continues to rally his troops, I return to the present, excited about the game.

"Leave it on the field, and play this game as if it will be your last one." Coach then steps aside as the team chaplain says a prayer for our safety.

"Amen." There is unity in our response.

Then—the butterflies. A call from the door indicates it's time to take the field, and the coaching staff decides the defense will lead us onto the field. The defensive unit is announced individually, one by one, as they run onto the field to be greeted by the stadium crowd and the national television audience. Eleven offensive players follow and, finally, the rest of us make our way to the sideline.

I am in awe! The stadium is sold out and overflowing with a standing room only crowd. Thousands of cameras flash in unison as we take the field, and the sidelines are lined with media and photographers who are here to capture the game in words and pictures—all while the cheerleaders are doing their thing to get the crowd excited!

I hear the fans screaming for their favorite players and, surprisingly, I spot the guy wearing the #20 jersey. He is still chanting, "Go, Cowboys," holding up his hand-made sign—he is so close, I can read his lips. I find it hard to believe he was so vocal and passionate for the past five hours! I do a double take to make certain he's the same guy—he is.

One last quick scan of the scene—as I stand on the sidelines, I notice the crowd's cheering. People are on their feet, clapping and hollering, and it sounds as if someone scored a touchdown or made an interception. Has the game already started without my knowing? I soon realize it isn't the sounds of the game I am hearing—it's a response by the crowd to a small group of people moving slowly up the east side of the field. One guy is in the middle of the group, but I can't make out his face. He is waving to the crowd and blowing kisses when his face suddenly flashes on the JumboTron, his name scrawled across the bottom of the screen—Garth Brooks! He slowly approaches the microphone set up at the fifty-yard line, his white ten gallon cowboy hat, blue jeans, and shirt mimicking the American flag. He punctuates the look with black cowboy boots and a silver belt buckle adorned with two pistols crossed on the barrel. He is definitely dressed for his role!

Both teams stand at full attention, the crowd silent. Millions of flashes of light spark throughout the stadium as Brooks starts to sing, the words clear and mesmerizing.

Three F-15 fighter jets fly low over the stadium, sending a chill throughout the crowd as Garth belts out *the rocket's red glare* . . . fireworks begin to explode in unison. He finishes to a fanatical cheer of appreciation from the crowd as he is escorted off the field.

I stand, contemplating what is happening. If the halftime show is anything like the opening, it will be a wonderful experience for the fans. One of my mother's favorite singers, Diana Ross, will perform, fulfilling two of my mother's dreams—seeing me in a Super Bowl, and seeing Diana Ross live, on stage.

The field crew cleans up the fireworks debris, and it's time for the captains of each team to meet in the middle of the field for the coin toss. We win and defer until the second half, per Coach Switzer's instructions—we are guaranteed to begin the second half with an offensive position.

"Kick-off team—you're up!" Our special teams coach signals the beginning of the game as our captain returns to the sidelines. Since I am a member of the kickoff unit, I grab my helmet and line up with the rest of the group. I huddle with the rest of the kicking team on the sideline while Coach takes a headcount to make sure everyone is present. Next, a brief motivational speech before breaking the huddle and lining up on the field to kick off.

Our opponent waits on the other side of the field. The whistle blows, and our kicker quickly acknowledges he is ready. He kicks, and we sprint down field to make the tackle. I notice, unfortunately, that my teammate to the right took off early, before the kick. I don't pay much attention because I figure he just got caught up in the excitement of the 'big stage.'

I'm not in a position to get in on the tackle—the

ball tracks to the other side of the field. My teammates, however, achieve our objective of downing the ball inside the twenty-yard line.

Flag. No surprise—he left early. But, that's okay because now I'll get a second chance to be in on the play. I refocus my thoughts on the reset to kick—this time, we down the ball on the twenty-seven yard line. It isn't what we want, and we turn the field over to the defense. The roar of the crowd surges as we trot off, the stadium electric with excitement.

Three up, three down. Punt.

Now it's our offense's game—their #1 efficiency rating in the leagued inspires confidence as we control the line of scrimmage.

First down. Stopped short. Punt.

The Steelers take over, again hitting our wall of defense. Punt.

This time, we move the ball downfield within field goal range—the kick is straight and true, and we are on the board with three points. I am excited because every time we walk away with points, it's another opportunity I have with our kickoff team. But, again, I don't have a chance to get in on a tackle.

The first quarter ends—Cowboys 3, Steelers 0.

The second quarter proves a different story—we score two touchdowns to their one, and the half ends with a score of 17-7 in favor of the Cowboys. As we prepare to leave the field, my only disappointment is I had two more chances to make plays in the first half, but both kickoffs sailed through the endzone with no chance of making a return.

Dallas fans are on their feet for a standing 'O' as we jog off the field for an extended halftime due to the extravagant performance by Diana Ross. The atmosphere in our locker room is positive, and we are excited about snagging the halftime lead. However, all good football teams know better than to get overly excited about a halftime lead—any shift in momentum can erase our advantage, sending it back to the Steelers.

We meet with our position coaches to find out if there are adjustments to the game plan. I reflect on my first-half play, and realized that up to this point, I hadn't played a single down on offense. My only opportunity was on special teams.

After the coaches meeting, we are free to move around as we please—we check in with trainers and equipment managers to treat injuries, re-tape ankles, adjust pads, and replace or repair our uniforms and helmets. I don't require special attention, so I retreat to my locker to reflect on the plays from the first half. As I visualize ways to make plays in the second half, my special teams coach stops by, patting me on the shoulder.

"Stay ready!"

"I am ready, Coach!"

Twelve-year veteran, Bill Bates, approaches me to offer a few pointers on how I can affect the second-half kickoffs, and, perhaps, make a tackle. We chatted, but, for the most part, I listen. I gesture a few times, letting him know I am paying attention. Although I agree with him on most of his advice, the rookie in me wants to think it through on my own. But, I vow to implement his pointers the next time we kick off.

Locker room traffic is still at a fast pace—coaches,

trainers, and players still trying to get things done. I sit quietly, waiting for our return to the field. As the time to take the field draws near, Coach Switzer calls the entire team together. It is a repeat of the meeting before the opening kickoff, and he gives a familiar halftime speech.

It's time for the second half.

Remnants of the halftime show are visible on the field, and surface conditions are compromised due to the show business extravaganza. The stadium seating areas resemble bees searching for nectar as the crowd returns to its seats, and stadium personnel work quickly to clear the field.

Kickoff.

We get a good return to the thirty-yard line, and I jog off as the offense takes the field.

First down. Incomplete pass.

Second down—a running play off the strong side of the line where we have two Pro Bowlers and future Hall of Famers. But, the defense reads the play well and, suddenly, the blocking breaks down. Three Steeler defenders break free, viciously hitting our veteran running back at the same time. Trainers rush to our star player as he remains motionless on the turf—he suffers injuries and, according to NFL rules, he has to be out of the game for at least one play.

"Williams, get in the game!" Coach Switzer orders.

I grab my helmet and run out to join the huddle.

Third and seven.

The offensive coordinator sends in the play—a short yardage pass play where I will have a free release into the flat. Just as the ball snaps, I notice the linebacker blitzing—I was the 'hot read.' I look quickly for the ball because our quarterback doesn't have much time for release. Sure enough, just as I turn my head to look back toward our QB, the ball is already in the air, coming my way.

A perfect throw allows me a catch, and I tuck the ball away without breaking my stride. Now in open field, I look up to see three Steeler defenders. As the first one nears, I put a signature 'shake' move on him—he gets close, but not close enough! He misses the tackle and face plants.

I keep running.

The second tackler closes fast, so I use a traditional spin move on him, leaving him grabbing for air. As I regain my balance, I see the third defender between the goal and me. I push myself to the limit, knowing it is going to be a footrace into the endzone. I streak down the sideline, the last defender chasing me and, without warning, everything goes blank.

The crowd falls silent.

My cleats pound the turf and from nowhere, I hear a clear voice yelling, "Go, Cowboys!" over and over again. The endzone looms, and the closer I get, the louder the voice. The Steelers strong safety is right behind me, desperately trying to run me down. I feel him closing the distance as I cross the ten-yard line.

The five-yard line.

I refuse to be denied. The screaming crowd is on its feet as I dive forward to launch myself into the endzone. Airborne, I feel a tap on my shoulder.

"Sleeping Beauty! It's time to get off the bus . . ."

I looked up at my teammate as he points out the window at a guy wearing a #20 Cowboy jersey, holding a sign reading, "Go, Cowboys—Kick Butt!"

"That guy's been going at it since we drove into the stadium," he told me as we prepared to exit the bus.

"Hey, Sherman! Sherman Williams! How about an autograph?" The guy recognized me.

"Sure! What do you want me to sign?"

"How about the back of my jersey?"

I expected to see Mel Renfro's or Ron Springs's name on the back of the jersey. But, there it was in bold letters.

S. WILLIAMS.

CHAPTER 2
Current Reality

On April 19, 2000, four years and three months after I reached the pinnacle of my sport earning a championship ring in Super Bowl XXX, the FBI took me into custody. Eight days later on April 27, 2000, the Grand Jury handed down an indictment, changing my life forever. I recall reading the indictment thinking, *what in the world could I have done to have the entire United States of America against me?* After all, I was recently a member of America's Team—how could they consider me the enemy? I had no criminal history, and I had never seen the inside of a jail!

I was photographed, finger printed, and ultimately stripped of my personal identity. I realized my birth name was no longer my primary source of identification, and I was reduced to a number—Inmate No. 07520-003. I tried to make sense of it all—the first five digits represent a sequential number issued within the region of the Federal District Court that indicted me. The last three digits indicate the metropolitan area or city of the state where I committed the alleged crime.

Honestly, the loss of my identity was the least of my worries. I sat in the Mobile, Alabama County Jail for six days prior to the Grand Jury indictment, and the impact of the criminal complaint hadn't sunk in—from day one, I was isolated from the general jail population. They put me in the infirmary where my access to family or friends was limited. No one could visit or call-in, and I was allowed only one phone call a day. The only real contact I had with anyone was with the white female prisoner directly across the hall from me. I don't remember her name, but I do remember she was there in state custody waiting for a court hearing due to some sort of violation. She told me she was previously arrested for petty theft, and sentenced to two years in prison. Since she was a repeat offender, she was used to being in the system.

We talked through our cell doors once in a while and, for the majority of my stay, we were the only two in the infirmary, but we never became friends. Up to that point, I couldn't speak to an attorney, although I did have an attorney who was working on a couple of civil matters for me. We had a decent rapport, but I wasn't completely satisfied with the outcome of the work he did for me. I wasn't sure if he were the right choice for handling my criminal defense case—stakes were high because I faced charges that might result in considerable Federal prison time.

Before long, I understood what it meant to lose my freedom. Once a day, the guard came to escort me to a shower and, after that, my one phone call. Although I obviously lost my criminal virginity, the once-a-day shower wasn't nearly enough to make me feel clean again.

During one of my conversations with the woman across the hall, she told me about her lawyer. She was satisfied with his work, and he worked out a favorable deal with her prosecutor. She was facing a ten-year sentence, but he negotiated a plea bargain that required serving two years with a possible early release for good behavior. Well, I figured if he could get a repeat offender such a sweet deal, he could surely get me bailed out of the claustrophobic county jail. I considered hiring him, but I failed to take one thing into consideration—she was State, I was Federal. Compared to the federal system, the state was lenient for reasons I don't understand.

I seized the opportunity during my next phone privilege to call my girlfriend—she was pregnant with my daughter, and I had no idea I would still be in jail when she was born. I was confident I would make bail, and be there for her birth. When I called, she was crying and upset—she was devastated I was still locked up without bail as well as the news of the indictment. She asked what she could do for me, and I gave her the phone number of the white woman's attorney. My girlfriend told me my mother already contacted my first attorney, and he was going to take care of it. I couldn't respond—if he were taking care of it, why was I still in jail? I asked her to make the call to the other attorney to see what he had to say. Then I told her I would call her back the following day.

Later that evening, I told the woman across the hall about the conversation with my girlfriend. From that point on, she tried to convince me of her attorney's expertise. Second thoughts crept in, and I wondered if she were chasing a referral fee when I heard one of the guards refer to him as "Cowboy Bob." The guard and the woman across the hall were surprised when I said I never heard of him.

Up until then, I didn't have any reason to hunt for or keep a list of criminal defense attorneys. I remembered a lawyer who handled a juvenile case for my mother—an experience during which I learned the value of having a good attorney. I was implicated in a second-degree gang related murder case that had no foundation and, thankfully, the lawyer got the case thrown out. Of course, I could have contacted him, but I wasn't sure he was the right attorney to handle my drug case. Besides, by this time, I was sold on Cowboy Bob—when I called my girlfriend the next day, I was surprised to find out she already spoke to him. Cowboy Bob told her he was aware of my case, and he was glad to provide a legal defense—all he needed was a $25,000 retainer.

A blessing, and a curse.

I didn't have $25,000 in liquid cash lying around, so I had to call my accountant to have him make the necessary withdrawal from one of my accounts. Yes, it was difficult, but not impossible, and I was worried I wouldn't have access to the money quickly. I figured the best strategy was to request my girlfriend to explain the situation to my good friend, David. I was certain he would step up to help me, but I hated to ask a friend for help. As it turned out, by the time I called my girlfriend again, David already sent the money to Cowboy Bob.

Bob's immediate task was to get me out of jail.

There's a part of me that wishes it wouldn't have happened like that—I would like to have had a chance to speak with Cowboy Bob and David before the money changed hands. I understand my girlfriend was acting out of care and concern, and she wanted me out of jail more than I did. I also know David would have asked me if the tables were turned. Nonetheless, Cowboy Bob was officially my attorney.

The following day, I was due in court for my arraignment and bail hearing. When I got there, many of my family and friends were already in the courtroom.

The magistrate judge was pleasant and soft spoken, and she didn't seem biased or prejudiced. The prosecutor was in her late forties or early fifties, and I think my case was the biggest in her career—she didn't have the experience to handle such a high-profile case. Keep in mind, my marijuana drug case wasn't that big—but, it was high profile and newsworthy because of my successful football career. Apparently, the U.S. Attorney's Office wanted her to achieve some success because she was the wife of the mayor of Mobile, Alabama. However, they didn't trust her to prosecute my case herself, and it was obvious because of the woman sitting next to her in court. Deborah Griffin was the Deputy Criminal Chief and head of the Narcotics Unit, and she was a well-known prosecutor who previously handled several high-profile cases in Mobile. Her role was as coach and advisor, and her name was enough to make the toughest drug dealer run for cover.

Not good.

Cowboy Bob and I met for the first time in the courtroom. He was a tall, heavy, older white man, his hair and beard a mix of grey and white. I immediately noticed he was excitable, and he reminded me of Santa Claus on meth. Since it was his first day on the case, the Feds knew he wouldn't be prepared to make a strong argument—it was their strategy. They wanted a hurry-up hearing, knowing I was at the full mercy of the court. Everything was done in due time, on their schedule.

The judge began to go through the standard procedures of the court—she asked questions such as, "Are you Sherman Williams?" "Are you competent to stand trial?"

"Do you understand what I am saying and reading?" Yes, yes, and yes. Next, she read each count of the indictment.

"How do you plead?"

"Not guilty."

I glanced around the courtroom and noticed David Fagan and Anthony Colderaro, the two detectives who arrested me a few days earlier—they were members of a low-level narcotics team recently established by the sheriff's office. The night they arrested me, they tried asking questions about the marijuana they found in their informant's apartment. As they interrogated me, I pretended to fall asleep and snore while I listened to the frustration in their voices.

It appeared they were still upset with me.

Colderaro was a tall guy who walked the room during my interrogation, making statements or shouting questions at me. Fagan, on the other hand, looked like a midget— he had an irritating, high-pitched voice, and he remained seated most of the time. Both used common scare tactics, threatening me with statements such as, "You know you're going to prison for thirty to forty years!" Or, "You can free yourself right now—just tell us what we want to know, and we'll let you go." Over and over, they repeated their threats to the point I did get bored and fell asleep! Finally, I asked if I were under arrest and, if so, would they please take me to jail. They didn't like that much, but, eventually, jail is where I wound up. They took great pride in bringing me down, and they sat with smug looks on their faces while the judge finished reading the indictment into the court record.

The next step was a bond hearing. It was Cowboy

Bob's job to make the case of why I should be allowed to post a bond, and to be released on bail until my trial date. My family and friends thought the proceedings were a formality because it was my first adult offense, and I didn't have a previous record.

I thought so, too.

Cowboy Bob began with the usual—I had significant family ties in the community, no outstanding warrants— the typical drill. He put my father on the stand to testify he would assume responsibility for providing a place for me to live in the local area. Yep, everything looked to be going my way . . .

"Bail denied!"

When the judge was asked why she made her decision, she replied, "Mr. Williams has in his possession a current passport, and the financial means to flee. Given the severity of his alleged offenses and the possibility of a long prison sentence, I consider him to be a flight risk." Unfortunately, Cowboy Bob lost round one, but I felt the fight was just beginning.

They took me back into custody, and transported me from court to the county jail. No infirmary this time— instead, they put me in a cellblock designed for violent prisoners, and those who violate the rules. It was also used to separate prisoners who have sensitive cases from the general jail population, or those who snitched on other prisoners in order to secure a lesser sentence. Criminals hate snitches, and they may be killed or severely injured in jail.

It took me a few days to adjust to PC (Protective Custody)—after all, it was my first rodeo. I was naïve about how things worked in the system, and everyone I met in PC told me things were better being locked up with the general jail population.

I soon found out why.

In PC, I was confined to a small cell for twenty-three hours of every day, and I was only given one hour outside of my cell to take a shower or use the phone. There was a day room where prisoners could play cards, watch T.V., or walk around to exercise and pass time, but I couldn't spend much time there. Meals made it to me three times a day through a slot in my cell door. Each meal was cold— breakfast consisted of milk, a biscuit, and a cup of grits. Lunch was pinto beans and collard greens, and dinner was a delicious bowl of chicken bones and rice. I was thankful when I found out I could spend forty dollars per week in the jail commissary which offered drinks, snacks, chips, and pastries. I learned I could increase my spending limit to sixty dollars a week by having other indigent prisoners buy twenty dollars' worth of items for me on their account. Since they had no source of income, I had someone outside make a forty-dollar weekly deposit into their account, and they would keep half. With the other half, they'd purchase a list of items for me.

It was a win-win situation.

Family and friends had no-contact visitation. Separated by a glass window, I spoke with them through an intercom telephone system. It was better than no visitation at all, but it always bothered me that our conversations were monitored. Because of that, I always took a pen and paper with me—whenever I wanted to keep something confidential, I wrote on the paper and held it up to the glass window for my visitor to read. No, it wasn't convenient, but that's how it went. Fortunately, when my attorney came to visit me a few weeks later, I learned we could talk face-to-face for an extended time.

Our first visit was okay—we talked about the indictment, and he explained what the charges meant, how much prison time I was facing, and the evidence against me. And, my chances to win at trial.

He told me there was video tape evidence.

"What video tape?" I was stunned. Cowboy Bob explained the Narcotics Unit set up a video camera in their informant's house, recording everything while I was there.

"Have you seen the tape?"

"Yes."

"Is it the only video they have?"

"Yes."

"If there are fifty pounds of marijuana in the informant's house, how can they indict me for distribution 1,000 pounds?"

"They have witness testimony—Demetrius Thomas. He swore before the Grand Jury you gave him over 1,000 pounds of marijuana over the last year."

"He's lying!" I was furious! "Okay—I admit to the fifty pounds on the video, but I'm going to fight the other claim of 1,000 pounds."

Cowboy Bob didn't flinch.

"Okay. Then we should prepare for trial . . ."

In shackles, I sat in the court holding area with Cowboy

Bob, and I asked if there were any chance of the judge changing her mind. He told me he would continue to try his best, but the court was unlikely to be responsive. The prosecutor told him there was a third suspect associated with my case, and they were still trying to track him down. His name was Roderick Ward—a person of interest identified by Demetrius Thomas and Frank Freeman— whom the FBI believed was implicated in the alleged drug conspiracy. It was clear until he were in custody, bail was out of the question. The mindset of the court was if I were allowed back on the street, I would continue my dealings with him—there was no way I could convince them otherwise.

My thoughts turned to the videos, and I asked my attorney if I could view them. I was also interested in reading a transcript of any statements made against me by my so-called co-conspirators. Cowboy Bob told me to be patient because he needed to file a Motion of Discovery in order to have unrestricted access to the tapes and transcripts. Learning that, I instructed him to move quickly so I could have the information as soon as possible. We shook hands, and one of the marshals escorted him from the courtroom holding area. They escorted me out, transporting me back to the county jail lock up.

When I returned my cellblock, prisoners greeted me with a great deal of curiosity. In any type of lockup, nothing happens without someone knowing about it—twenty-four hours a day, the place is all eyes and ears. Whenever I left, the prisoners left behind wanted to know where I was going and why. They seem to have a voice of great concern, but, in reality, we were so isolated from everyday society that natural curiosity prevailed.

County jail in Mobile, like most jails across America, is

a small community of men confined to a small space or pod, and everybody wants to know everyone else's business. The truth is there was a strange feeling associated with being in jail for the first time—it was nothing like anything else I experienced in my life. Even though I knew my fellow prisoners for a short period of time, it seemed as if bonding were almost instantaneous. I think it's because there was a sense of 'we're in this together' . . .

Ours was a small, eclectic group of characters—the old man, Frank, was a black man in his mid-50s. He reminded me of the stereotypical old military veteran who lost his mind in the war. I think the only reason he was in the PC cellblock was because he was crazy, and couldn't function in the general population.

Then there was Mr. Johnson—an older, white gentleman who was a big college football fan, and he recognized me from my playing days at the University of Alabama. An airplane pilot from the Talladega area, he was a repeat offender caught trying to smuggle marijuana on a flight from Mexico to the U.S. He reminded me of the '70s hippie type—hollow eyes surrounded by deep wrinkles, and stringy hair brushing his collar. Despite his appearance, he seemed an intelligent man.

Within the group, Mr. Johnson and I were the most talkative, but direct conversation was limited because we were in one-man cells. Although he seemed to express genuine concern about my case, I was suspicious about him. I thought he might be a snitch for the Assistant U.S. Attorney, and I was warned by others not to say anything to him about my case. It wasn't uncommon for snitches to be planted in a pod in order to secure inside information about a particular case. A snitch could get valuable information for the prosecution, and, perhaps, receive a reduced sentence for his testimony.

Mr. Johnson had knowledge about how the federal system worked, and he and I were the only two men in the pod with federal charges. He constantly asked me things such as, "What's your lawyer telling you about your chances of getting out?" Or, "What kind of evidence do they have on you?" When I told Mr. Johnson I was preparing to go to trial, he tried to convince me going to trial was a mistake. He was a repeat offender awaiting sentencing, and I think he knew his only hope was a plea bargain. I felt my case was different—especially after he confided in me his incarceration for was his third offense, and it wasn't long since the second.

Another character was Mr. Marcus—he was a quiet, paranoid personality type, and suspicious of the relationship Mr. Johnson and I developed. He was in the county jail after being indicted for allegedly murdering his wife and burning her body in a car fire in order to collect the life insurance. I quickly learned why Mr. Marcus was so quiet and suspicious of Mr. Johnson's relationship with me—his former 'cellie' told prosecutors Mr. Marcus confessed to him. Obviously, Mr. Marcus should have kept his mouth shut! Although the prosecution would use the snitch as their key witness against Mr. Marcus, it always presented the prosecution with a dilemma as to the credibility of the witness because he was a criminal. Keeping quiet about the details of my case prior to trial was a lesson learned, and one I would not soon forget.

Time passed, and Mr. Johnson and Mr. Marcus were sentenced and gone. Johnson got ten years, and Marcus received the death penalty. It was June, I was still sitting in the county jail, and several more characters came and went. My girlfriend was due to give birth to our beautiful baby girl. The trial hadn't occurred yet, and I wanted to be present for the birth of my daughter, so I began to petition the court for another bond hearing. I offered to put up all of my earthly possessions as security against flight risk—a million bucks' worth.

Petition denied.

Time for a new strategy. Since I was getting nowhere with the court, I began to write to the warden. My intent was to explain my current situation and emphasize I had no criminal history. My hope was he had a family of his own, and he would be sympathetic to my request to be present at the birth of my daughter. Eventually, the warden informed me he couldn't let me leave the jail, but he would set up a contact visit for me after the birth. My girlfriend and the baby would be allowed visitation in a private room where we could hug and kiss, and I could hold the baby— all supervised by one of the lieutenants.

When the visit occurred, it only lasted one hour—to me, it seemed like a few minutes. But, I was grateful to be given such an opportunity by the warden. After the visit ended, I returned to my cell and cried, realizing what I already missed. Finally, the reality of my situation tumbled down on me—I was in big trouble, and it appeared there wasn't anything a lawyer or I could do about it!

Everyone has at least one defining moment—for me, jail was it. I had to get back to my roots, so I grabbed the Holy Bible from the book cart, and I soon discovered there were a few guys who also had bibles. We talked about Christ and the gospel and, as the days went by, the Bible provided a positive focus by preventing me from being consumed by the negative circumstances surrounding me.

Several more weeks passed without any contact

with Cowboy Bob, and it left me with the impression that no work was being done. I received notice in the mail indicating a trial date was set, and then I received another notification indicating the date changed at the request of my attorney. So, I tried to contact them to find out what was going on, and several more weeks passed with no reply. I found solace by understanding why I was housed in protective custody instead of integrated with the general population—it was due to my social status as a prominent University of Alabama and NFL athlete. Yet, I didn't feel I needed isolation.

I grew up in Prichard, Alabama—a poor, predominantly black community with a significant amount of violent crime in the streets. Since I survived that experience, I was sure I could handle the young thugs in the county jail—in fact, I was sure the majority of them were from Prichard, too. So, I wrote to the judge, warden, and the marshall's office requesting to be placed in the general population. I always thought of myself as a nonviolent man, but after four to five months of being isolated from humanity for twenty-three hours each day, the frustration began to build and the daily routine was boring. I felt as if I were going crazy, so it was no surprise that by the sixth month I was involved in my first fistfight.

The guy was one of those bully types named Rick—he was about three to four years older than I, and a couple of inches taller. However, I outweighed him by ten to fifteen pounds. He was in PC because he ticked off some of the dudes in the general population, and they threatened him with bodily harm. Well, he caught me on one of those days when things weren't going well—although I was studying the Bible, I hadn't gotten to the point I needed to reach. God was patient, but I wasn't.

It started with a phone call.

I was in the middle of a phone conversation as Rick waited in line. He rudely interrupted my conversation, and told me to hurry up and get off the phone. I shot him a 'who do you think you are' look, and continued with my call.

It didn't work. Luckily, the backdrop behind the wall phone was made of stainless steel, reflecting much like a mirror. As I faced it, I watched Rick while I continued my conversation—sure enough, he was approaching me. As he got to within arms' reach, I pivoted toward him.

"What's your problem?" I cupped my hand over the receiver as I confronted him.

"Phone check, Homey!"

I politely told my friend on the phone to hang on for a second and, in one motion, I cracked Rick across his head with the receiver part of the phone.

Then I body slammed him to the floor.

We rolled around on the floor for a few minutes, pointing at each other until the guards intervened. As they pulled us apart, I noticed blood coming from the spot where I split Rick's head open with the phone. "This isn't over!" he shouted from across the room. I watched the guards remove him from the room while I offered no resistance.

They wasted no time in moving me to the next pod after allowing me a few minutes to gather my things. Unfortunately, the next pod over was so full that some of the men were sharing cells. Although I wanted my own cell, I was put in a cell with a white guy named Jeremy Bentley—he and I were the same age, but that was the only thing we had in common. Jeremy was facing a capital murder charge—if found guilty, he would receive life without parole, or the death penalty. He told me his co-defendant was in the pod I just left, and I mentioned I heard the story, but didn't know the facts. As his new cellie, I knew there was plenty of time to hear the details.

It turns out Jeremy was a pretty cool guy. I felt for him because of the position he was in—his case was a robbery-homicide. Since the crime consisted of two felonies committed during the act of a murder, it was likely to end in the death penalty. But, as the saying goes, God works in mysterious ways. Jeremy believed in God, and we often shared our thoughts and views of the Bible. Our interests and beliefs made time spent in isolation more palatable—and, for a time, I had someone I could bounce my thoughts off while locked down for twenty-three hours a day. To our luck, we managed to get our hands on a chessboard, and we became fierce competitors. If he were here today, he would testify the final score of our chess competition was 1,139 to 943 in my favor—all in all, we played over 2000 matches! I guess you could say I became a pretty decent chess player . . .

After spending six months in the slammer, Cowboy Bob visited me a couple of times—he chalked his lack of appearances up to preparing for trial, which was only two weeks away. I learned he hired an assistant, Arthur Madden, to help me with my case, and he was the type of lawyer who knew the details and procedures of the law very well.

I thought he was a nerd.

On the other hand, Cowboy Bob was an animated orator, so I could understand why he hired him. Two weeks before trial, Madden came to see me, plea bargain in hand, requiring me to spend more time in jail. Of course, it wasn't what I wanted to hear, and I told him to go back and work out a deal whereby I would be released from jail immediately. I was convinced I served more than enough time in jail, but he was adamant the plea bargain was the best he could do. So, I told him to continue preparing for trial—I also asked him how things were looking, and he said it looked like it was coming down to a roll of the dice! I told him I was fully aware if I accepted the plea bargain there was no way I could avoid jail time.

I told him to strike the Plea Agreement.

Time passed. Cowboy Bob and Arthur worked on my defense, and we finally reached a tipping point when it was time to seat a jury. No turning back. I wasn't involved in the whole process, but eventually they notified me the jury was selected. For me, the trial was equivalent to game time—a time when all of our preparation and hard work would pay dividends.

On the first day of my trial, it was the first time I saw the jury. It was a diverse group of fourteen individuals— twelve jurors and two alternates. Our judicial system called it a jury of my peers, but as I scanned the jury seated in the courtroom, I couldn't help but wonder if the fifty-year-old white woman were one of my peers.

The jury was a mix of ten male and female Caucasians, plus one black male, and one black female—the alternates were black females. Cowboy Bob and Arthur were satisfied with the makeup of the jury, but I wasn't so sure since my defense was entirely in their hands. However, I had no choice but to have faith in their opinion—then, as quickly as the trial started, it ended!

Immediately after both sides made opening statements, the judge declared a mistrial. The reason had something to do with juror misconduct, and I was never sure why the mistrial occurred. But, I began to think it was a part of a bigger strategy for the prosecution, and I viewed it as an attempt to overcome the obviously weak case they had against me.

Turned out Judge Lee was removed from my case and it was then in the hands of Judge Vollmer—an older, white man who seemed to possess a strong personality. It was my thought that federal judges don't typically declare a mistrial so early in the proceedings unless they feel strongly something is amiss—so, everyone met in the judge's chamber after he declared the mistrial. I was silent as Judge Vollmer gave instructions to the attorneys regarding how they should proceed and, after everyone agreed on a new trial date, I leaned over to Cowboy Bob and told him to push for another bail hearing.

It never happened.

Patsy Dow was still the lead prosecutor on my case, although Deborah Griffin sat by her side the entire time. The consensus of my defense team was my trial was too high profile for the Justice Department to rely on an inexperienced Ms. Dow as the prosecutor. They really didn't want my case to go to trial—but, they really didn't have any choice because I had no intention of accepting any plea deal they offered.

The Justice Department has unlimited resources, and even when a drug case was already in the court system, they continued to build a list of co-conspirators. It figures— after the mistrial, I learned they brought charges against one of my good friends, Kenneth Rice, as well as his friend, Ricky Mason. Apparently, Frank Freeman (the snitch who cooperated with the Feds to set up the sting resulting in my arrest), also named Rice and Mason as part of the drug distribution conspiracy. To this day, it still amazes me Rice and Mason were indicted strictly on statements made by Freeman with no other evidence against them!

By this time, I was beginning to wear down, and I started to think about a plea agreement. I knew the prosecution wanted to interview me to find out how much additional information I might provide regarding the source of the fifty pounds of marijuana they found at Freeman's house. Still, I didn't speak to them.

After we left Judge Vollmer's chambers, I told Cowboy Bob I would consider admitting knowledge of the fifty pounds of marijuana documented on the videotape—Count 1. However, the prosecution would have to agree to drop Counts 2 and 3, and accept the fact I wouldn't cooperate any further with the FBI. It was against my personal values to provide any information leading to the arrest of other people in order to obtain a lesser sentence or fine for myself. Besides, there weren't any guarantees made by the prosecution, even if I did cooperate.

They transported me back to the county jail, and I returned to my cell. I was glad to be back, and to have a chance to vent my frustrations to Jeremy. He was patient, a good listener, and we talked through the night—I really appreciated having him as my cellie. We agreed the mistrial was a sign from God, and I needed to stay strong and be patient—soon, I would be home. We also agreed there were positive outcomes of the mistrial—we got to see all of the prosecution's evidence against me, as well as a list of the witnesses who would testify against me at trial.

Time passed slowly in the county jail, but after a few weeks Cowboy Bob and Arthur came to see me. They went over the evidence with me again, and it was clear they had the video of Frank Freeman and me at his apartment—plus, various statements from Freeman, Roderick Ward,

Demetrius Thomas, Demetria Bean, and Terence Ball that would be used against me.

Terrance Ball? Who? I never heard his name, or met anyone by that name in my entire life! My attorney told me Ball made a statement to the FBI that he knew me well, and we did drug deals together.

I was furious!

As I reviewed the list of witnesses, I discovered a couple of names of people whom I didn't know, including Anthony King, and Eddie Savage. It appears it's common practice for the FBI to generate a list of co-conspirators in a drug conspiracy case simply because someone named names. There is no hard evidence of wrongdoing needed—in fact, it occurred to me the Justice Department promotes a 'guilty until proven innocent' doctrine to indict defendants. It clearly violated the presumption of innocence doctrine that is the foundation of the American judicial system.

As we continued to talk about moving forward with the trial, Arthur asked if I might be willing to consider a plea deal based on what we knew. I agreed, but only for Count 1—Demetrius Thomas was lying about the 1000 pounds, and I wasn't going to plead guilty to something I didn't do.

I tried to change the subject back to another bail hearing, but Cowboy Bob said they weren't going to give me one, and we ended our meeting on a low note. By that time I was mentally whipped, so I went back to my cell and took a nap. When I woke up, I thought about everything we discussed, and I was certain of only one conclusion—I was ready to get out of that hellhole!

When it was time for my next phone call, I called my

family. I instructed my mother to call Arthur to tell him to work out a plea deal that would get me out of there. She said okay, and a few days later I had a visit from Cowboy Bob. He had the plea deal in his briefcase and, as he handed it to me, he indicated it was the best we were going to do.

I read through the Plea Agreement, and I didn't like it. The 1,000 pounds of marijuana was reduced to 226 pounds, and they added a gun charge plus two kilos of cocaine. I jumped all over Cowboy Bob, demanding answers. What gun? What cocaine? How did the 1,000 pounds turn into 226 pounds? He told me Kenny Warmon made a statement—in the past he'd seen me with a gun. What? I immediately asked what that had to do with anything! Then Cowboy Bob told me I was being charged with distribution of two kilos of cocaine because Frank 'the snitch' Freeman said I told him to get it. However, in terms of the original indictment, no one could explain to me how fifty pounds of marijuana turned into 226 pounds.

The Plea Agreement I had in my hand also required me to pay the government $190,000—a court fine purportedly equal to the drug proceeds from the alleged sale. The final condition of the plea agreement required me to accept responsibility and serve forty-seven months in prison. I wasn't happy with these conditions, and I didn't hesitate for one second to instruct Cowboy Bob to tell Deborah and her staff, thanks, but no thanks.

I had to calm down. I turned back to Cowboy Bob and asked if I went to trial and lost, what did he foresee as the outcome.

"Anywhere from ten to fifteen years."

A punch in the gut.

"What if I accept this plea, and refuse to cooperate with the Feds? How much time do you think I'll face then?"

Cowboy Bob didn't need to think about his answer.

"The same—ten to fifteen years."

I asked him for a copy of the Plea Agreement, and told him I would go back to my cell to read it. By this time, I concluded my only option was to proceed with trial—but, I needed time to think.

"Don't take too long, because we don't want to lose the deal. The faster you decide, the sooner we'll know what we need to do from this point on." Cowboy Bob was matter-of-fact, as if my life were already decided.

As I waited for the guard to escort me back to lockup, I felt hopeless. I was trying to fight the full force of the United States Justice Department from the inside of a tiny jail cell—no access to a law library, the Internet, or other resources. Although I had faith in my attorneys, communication between the three of us was limited, and I had no available resources to assist in my own defense in the effort to win my freedom. All of the advantage and momentum was in favor of the prosecution. They had unlimited resources to make an innocent person look guilty—they not only had the power of the Federal court behind them, they also used media sources to prosecute me in the court of public opinion. Let's face it—the average citizen can't possibly afford the legal costs to mount a strong defense—it's the main reason they carry a 99% conviction rate, and most cases plea-bargain out.

While I was sitting in the county lockup, the FBI was out and about interviewing anyone who knew me well, or was in some way associated with me. Childhood friends.

Ex-girlfriends. College teammates. They sought anybody able to provide information to strengthen their case against me and, in some strange way, it gave me hope their case against me was weaker than I thought. By the time they were finished with their interviews, they interviewed over fifty people and, eventually, they narrowed the list down to only four who were willing to provide information to help make their case against me. I mentioned their names before—Roderick Ward, Demetrius Thomas, Frank Freeman, and Demetria Bean. Ward and Freeman were so-called friends from my childhood in Prichard, and Thomas was an employee at Shake 20 Productions, my recording studio. Bean was a stripper I met in the Dallas Metroplex area.

The case broke on March 4, 2000 when the FBI—in conjunction with DEA—arrested Thomas. At the time of the arrest, he was carrying a nine millimeter pistol, and three pounds of marijuana. Since there was no way he could talk himself out of a bad situation, he immediately coughed up info for the Feds. It's also when the half-truths and lies started, and he lied to the FBI claiming he bought 1000 pounds of marijuana from me. I learned Demetrius Sanders, a friend of Thomas, was with him at the time of the arrest. He stopped by Shake 20 to tell me what happened, and he said he and Thomas were interrogated in separate rooms. Sanders was more than suspicious Thomas was working with the Feds . . . me, too.

I eventually learned Thomas snitched on Ward and Bean and, in addition, he told them my girlfriend would back up their story. That was all they needed, and the Feds threatened to indict her if she didn't cooperate. I couldn't let that happen, so I put up $5,000 for an attorney to represent her—recommended by Cowboy Bob—and I needed to hire a lawyer who was a colleague of his so I could be informed of my girlfriend's situation. It proved to be a good move on my part, because it provided confidence and comfort to her—she refused to cooperate, and she never broke during the duration of my case.

When I returned to the pod, I asked the guard for my hour outside of my cell—I wanted to call my girlfriend as soon as possible to share the information my attorney gave me while it was still fresh in my mind. The guard granted my request, and I was glad I called because my mother was with her at the time. It gave me a chance to receive feedback and input from both of them regarding the plea agreement. I explained the plea agreement would require me to spend at least forty-seven months in prison. In addition, I would have to cooperate with them—meaning, I would agree to everything Freeman, Thomas, and Ward said was true. It also set up a worst-case scenario, where I may have to testify against Kenneth Rice and my girlfriend.

"I know you, Sherman—if you agree to this plea bargain and testify against others on behalf of the prosecution, you'll never get over the guilt. The four years you spend in prison will seem like you are doing fifteen years." My girlfriend was right. I couldn't live with myself knowing I was a snitch—it was against my values, and it wasn't cool. Besides, my mother said going to trial was the only option, and she wanted me to win my trial so I could go home.

When I hung up, I immediately went back to my cell to share my thoughts with Jeremy. He gave me advice, realizing that in the end I was the only one who could make the decision. So I lay down on my bunk, contemplating my options throughout the night. Eventually, I got on my knees and prayed to God—I trusted in Him, and I left everything in His hands.

The following day, I called my girlfriend while she was

still at my mother's house to tell her my decision. I told her I wasn't going to accept the plea offer, and she and my mother agreed. So, I asked her to call Cowboy Bob, and tell him to come see me. I also told her not to tell him. I made a decision . . .

Twenty-four hours later, he showed up.

We met in the usual spot, and I didn't waste time telling him I wasn't taking the plea, and that I wanted him to focus all of his time and energy on the preparation of my trial. I believed we wouldn't be able to seat a jury in Mobile that wasn't tainted by the media coverage of my case, so I asked for him to draft and file a Motion for Change of Venue.

That day we began to prepare aggressively for my trial.

Chapter 3
Ground Zero—the Home Field

My parents married at an early age because Mom was pregnant with my older brother while she was still in high school. As with most teenage pregnancies, it wasn't a good thing and it forced her to leave high school to attend an alternative school—her only option for graduating with her diploma. Life was tough, but it didn't stop her from getting her education because she was determined to be an educated mom.

Encouraged to do the right thing, my father graduated from high school, got a job, and married my mother. He committed to his wife and child, just as his father did for my grandmother and their three children when they settled in Prichard, Alabama. But, throughout the years, my parents endured a dysfunctional marriage, and it wasn't until they had three children that I came into the picture—I was born Sherman Cedric Williams on August 13, 1973, the youngest of four children.

Prichard is a small, predominantly African-American town of approximately 33,000 people and, in the late '60s and early '70s, the Civil Rights Movement was in its early stages, racial unrest coursing through the town. One of the good things to come out of the movement was jobs were plentiful—my father worked for International Paper Mill, Prichard's largest manufacturer. His job came with perks—great benefits and a retirement plan—and both were blessings since it wasn't common for a woman to have a job. Mom was no different—my father was the breadwinner while she stayed home and, by the time I came along, my parents were married for eight years.

Growing up, home was a one-way street in the heart of Prichard—just one street over from the Prichard Stadium where I would eventually play my high school football games. As a kid, Prichard wasn't the most exciting life, but we always found something to do. I didn't know what decisions would face me later—I was a happy kid, and I looked forward to being a big kid who went to school. When I was six, the Board of Education temporarily moved grades one through five to a different school, and I was one of the kids who was bussed. By second grade, I was back at my original elementary school getting into trouble! Often! I was a regular in the principal's office, but my grades were pretty good, so I passed to the third grade—the same year my mother and father divorced.

Mom did well for herself on her own. Prichard turned ghetto, and it was as crime infested as any ghetto community across America. Even with the moral values instilled by my grandfather during their upbringing, my aunts and uncles engaged in criminal activity. I had so many negative role models and influences in my life that I became a rebel myself. Behavior problems surfaced when I started school, escalating because with my dad out of the picture, I didn't have a solid role model. The school called Mom on numerous occasions, and I began to exhibit signs of violent behavior by fighting with schoolmates.

It was natural I looked to my older brother for guidance—as a senior in high school, he was the closest thing to a father I had in my life. His friends were athletes, and it wasn't too long after they started hanging out in our backyard lifting weights that I realized football was in my genes. I was a scrawny kid, but the sport interested me and, when we watched the pro games on T.V,, I knew playing football was something I wanted to do. After watching my brother and his friends, I asked him if I could lift weights with him—most of the time he said no. He and his friends laughed at me, telling me to get out of the way—so I'd stand aside and watch. Once in a while, they rewarded my patience by asking me to pass them a weight or two.

There were always footballs lying around in the backyard, so while they lifted weights, I started organizing the neighborhood kids to play a few pickup games. Even though I wasn't allowed to lift weights with them, they let me play with the footballs as much as I liked. During these games, I emulated plays I saw on T.V., or while I was watching one of my brother's games. Of course, I had no idea of what I was doing, but by the time his football season started, I taught myself how to catch a football pretty well—and, I discovered I had a natural talent for running.

By the end of my brother's last high school football season, I was running and catching the football well for someone my age. But, there was one thing I couldn't improve upon—my size.

I was still one of the smallest kids in my age group.

****

That year for Christmas I asked my mother to buy me a football and basketball, and she did. She arranged to have a basketball hoop put up in our backyard, and I think she was hoping if I could expend more energy on sports, my behavior at school would change. It helped, no doubt, but it wasn't a total cure.

That fall I focused on football and, when the season ended, I turned my attention to basketball. No, it wasn't the sport I loved, but it occupied my time. I looked forward to the opening game in September, and I kept up my running and throwing chops during the spring and summer. As I increased my skill in football and basketball, I figured I was ready.

I was ready for my own set of weights.

I asked my mother to buy them for my ninth birthday and, when the big day came, I was the owner of a brand-new, cement grey set. I couldn't wait to get started on my new exercise regimen, but I must have discovered early on that lifting weights was work. I hardly used them. I know she spent hard-earned money on them and, later, I felt guilty—I guess I learned the hard way I wasn't going to be able to do the things my brother did as an eighteen-year-old high school senior when I was only a nine-year-old fourth grader!

****

As I graduated from one grade to another, one thing I learned about myself was second place wasn't good enough. I was (and, am) competitive, and my competitive nature got me into trouble at school. Since I was small for my age, I carried a chip on my shoulder—I thought the only way to earn respect was to get into fights, and I didn't figure out until much later I was overcompensating for my size, as well as the emotional hurt of my family situation. I needed an outlet for my energy, and there was only one thing that made me truly happy.

Football.

I put all of my excess energy into the sport, playing games with my weekend endzone team at the high school games. I also played with some of the older guys in my neighborhood—grass fields. Dirt roads. Empty streets. It didn't matter—we played whenever, and wherever. My adolescence surged, I developed my own identity, noticed girls at school, and linked up with my first neighborhood crew, The Youngsters.

What could be better?

I felt strong and accepted by my crew members— Randal (he lived across the street), Leon (he lived behind me), and Bobby (who lived next door to Randal). Most of the time we got along well, and we met every morning to walk to school together. Like most kids, we occasionally had a falling out and we'd fight among ourselves—but, the truth was we were just little boys doing what little boys do.

During my elementary school years, my focus was on sports, and my mother kept me in check by setting down rules. Unless I did my chores and homework after school, there was no football with the guys. It was the same for the others, too, so we pushed each other to take care of our responsibilities at home as quickly as possible so we could hook up.

I made every effort to be as accomplished as possible. Each year I worked harder than the previous year, and I recognized my progress as I saw my body develop. I was still small, but I possessed a sense of skill in sports not usually noticed in a kid my age. My focus kept me on track most of the time, and I began to set my sights on bigger and better things. I played park leagues each summer and fall, and I was ready to go for something bigger and better.

And that's the way things went until I entered Junior High School—I kept increasing my football chops, as well as other seasonal sports.

But, football was always my number one.

Chapter 4
Gangs vs. Games

Every year in January, Mobile hosted a college all-star football game called the Senior Bowl. I went a few times with my family, but when I was in seventh grade my mom allowed me to go with some of the older guys from our neighborhood. I was excited to be hanging out with them, so I shouldn't have been surprised when they decided to take something with them to warm their bones. January is normally the coldest month of the year in Mobile, so on our way to the game the older guys stopped by the liquor store to pick up some alcohol. They said it was for keeping us warm during the game and, since I was pretty darned cold, I figured if it kept them warm it would keep me warm, too!

I don't think I'll ever forget what happened after we left that liquor store . . . we piled into the car and headed out for the game and, on the way to the stadium, they were pouring drinks and smoking cigarettes. I couldn't just sit there in the backseat, so joining the action seemed the right thing to do. I asked for a cupful of some of the 'good stuff,' and they didn't hesitate to give it to me.

I downed it like ice water on a hot summer day.

When I asked for a refill, they advised me to slow down, but I drank the second cup and asked for a third. The third was my last—I remember getting out of the car and walking to our seats, but I don't remember a thing after that. The next time I opened my eyes, it was halftime.

I awakened in a pool of vomit, and my sister was standing over me yelling, "What's wrong with you, Boy?" She was very upset because she was at the game with her boyfriend, and they had to leave to take me home. They dropped me off, returned to the game, and when Mom got home I was in bed with a slight headache. Thank God she didn't come home earlier! It was best not to have an in-depth conversation with her right then about my 'illness,' and I suspected my sister couldn't wait to tell Mom, anyway.

I was right.

As usual, my sister blabbed to my mother about everything, but she didn't know I was drinking—the guys at the game told her I started throwing up after eating some bad food. When my mother questioned me, I repeated the same story and, fortunately, she believed me. The next time I got together with the guys, they teased me about getting drunk—it was a good learning experience for me, and I gained their respect. From that point on, I continued to hang around with them.

****

Spring inched nearer and, as a seventh grader, I was eligible to attend the spring prom for the first time. There was a big transition from sixth to seventh grade, and I could attend more school events. Girls were on my mind, and I wanted to find one to ask to the spring prom—it was getting closer and I knew I was going, but I wasn't confident I could get a date. My crew and I discussed potential candidates, and I thought about asking a particular girl, but she already declined to be my girlfriend. She also attended a different school, and had a strict mother who didn't allow her to socialize with boys—that's when I began to think about Kiesha. She was a pretty girl in my class, and she always treated me nicely. Light-skinned with long hair, I thought she looked like an Indian girl in a Western movie.

I'm not sure, but it might have been fate when we crossed paths on Easter Sunday. In Prichard, it was a big deal for people of all ages to hang out at Will Park on Easter and, from my perspective, it seemed as if the entire black population were there. By then, Randal and I still hadn't found a date, and that's when I ran into Kiesha. After a few minutes of seventh grader small talk, she introduced me to her mother—apparently, she had already told her mother about me because she introduced me as 'Sherman Williams, the funny boy in my class.' I wondered if she told her mother about some of my classroom antics that got me disciplined, and labeled the class clown.

As nice as her family was, it seemed the best thing for us to do was to break off from them, so we went over to the monkey bars and I decided to pop the question.

"Are you going to the prom?"

"Yes."

"Do you have a date?"

"No . . ." When she said no, I got excited since the next question would be the most important.

"Will you go with me?"

"Yes!"

Things were lookin' good! I was well on my way to stepping up and filling my big brother's shoes! I was in organized sports, and I had a good start on a brand-new girlfriend. The only thing left to do was to start lifting weights to build up my body. But, as before, there was something about weightlifting I didn't like . . .

****

Time passed, the school year was over, and it was a pretty good year for me. Socially, I was well known around school and I had two girlfriends. I was more involved in school activities, my grades were good, and I passed to the next grade. However, my personal conduct was still a work in progress.

The summer of 1986 was pretty normal, and I tried to fill the time by continuing to play sports and training for the park football leagues. I began to make a name for myself, but, like most summers in Prichard, training and playing football weren't enough to keep me out of trouble. Growing up, my mother always told me not to allow anyone to ride my bike because they would ride off never to be seen again. I knew she was right—but, I also recognized the opportunity to make a buck. The sad thing was I had a growing gang mentality, so I tried to convince my crew that we should steal bikes, or spare parts. Randal and Leon didn't want any part of it, but Bobby and I got real tight that summer—bicycle capers. I ended up having so many different bicycle parts in my possession that I became a neighborhood bicycle mechanic. My first entrepreneurial venture brought parents and kids from the neighborhood in search of a bike mechanic, but it wasn't what it seemed— my repair business also served as a cover for when my mother would ask how I got so many accessories for my bike. Bobby and I had the coolest bikes in the neighborhood—of anyone our age—decorated with reflectors and streamers. My cover made sense, and I explained my capers to my mother as a legitimate business.

But, as the saying goes, *all good things must come to an end.* Halfway through the summer, my mom found out what I was doing. Turned out one of my customers owned of one of the bikes Bobby and I kyped. He told his parents he saw his stolen bike at my place, and they called my mother to make arrangements to come over and check it out. When they matched the serial number I was busted, my mother was furious, and my operation shut down. I escaped serious punishment because there was no proof I actually stole the bike. Nonetheless, my mother made me get rid of every bicycle part, and that ended my so-called business. I was lucky to get off so easy, and I even got to keep my bike and all the stuff I put on it.

After the unfortunate demise of my business, my crew and I found our ways back to the sandlot games. By now, I was a legitimate player, but I still had a hard time tackling the older and bigger guys. So, I thought if I were going to play for the school, I needed to start lifting weights. Again. That's when I started to spend more time at my friend's house, and that's when I met his older brother. He recently moved back to his mother's house—he didn't go to school, or have a job—and he just hung around. Every time I saw him, he had a cigarette in his mouth and a brown paper bag containing a cheap bottle of wine in his hand. He was cool and funny, always enjoying acting like a comedian and making fun of me when I tried to lift weights. I always came up short. One day, he was half drunk, smoking a cigarette, and no plans to do anything. I asked if I could have a cigarette, and he offered one along with a light. I smoked once before while messing around with my cousin Patrick at my grandmother's house, and it made me sick. This time, I smoked a cigarette like a pro with no ill effects. For some reason the act of smoking without hacking myself to death served as a bonding agent for my new friend and me, and I found myself hanging out with him often. The next time I asked him for cigarette, he reached into his shirt pocket and pulled out something looking similar to a cigarette, but different. Before I could ask what was, he said, "You would have to smoke 12 cigarettes to get what you can get out of just one of these!"

"What is it?"

"A joint! But, when it comes to marijuana, you're gonna have to find your own."

He explained dollar joints and nickel bags were popular, and both were easy to score in the hood. Being thirsty for male guidance, I began to walk down his path. I thought he was what I needed—he was older, wiser, and he treated me like an equal without considering my age. Well, I began to spend some of my money made on the bicycle hustle on cigarettes and wine—but, despite all of my wasted time, I still found enough time to play in the neighborhood football games. After the games, the older guys kicked back, telling war stories while downing a few beers. Now? I was now an experienced drinker,and I wasn't afraid to ask for one.

****

Coach Marshall. A big, burly guy who talked like a drill sergeant. Not only was he always yelling and screaming, he had a strange way of putting his team together. He used what he called 'Challenge for Positions.' Out of the twenty-two positions making up the offense and defense for his park league, I could challenge any of them. The only rule was the guys who returned from the year before had priority, and they usually claimed their positions from the previous year. That is, unless someone challenged them and took it away.

My friend, Michael, played opposite running back the year before when I was playing for the EIGHTMILE league. At that time, my preference was to play defense, and there were a few defensive spots available. So, I decided to challenge for one of the cornerback positions. The challenge was based on 'last man standing' drill—two challengers lined up about thirty yards apart, and ran full speed until they met somewhere in the middle. The goal was to drag my opponent across the line I defended and, if I accomplished the goal, I moved on to the next round until there was only one man left standing. At that point, the winner won the position.

I was one of three guys competing for cornerback, so we drew straws to see who would go first—I lost. So, I needed to win twice in order to earn the position. When I lined up for the first round, I was confident in my skills, but not so confident about my size and strength compared to my opponents. Luckily, other guys went before me for different positions, so I had a chance to think up a strategy. By the time Coach called my name, I had it worked out my head—the only things both of my opponents had in their favor were size and weight.

We lined up on the field, and proceeded to run full

speed at each other until we made contact. I thought I drew a tough opponent, and I braced myself. Much to my surprise, he immediately sailed backward and seemed disoriented. So, I seized the opportunity to quickly drive forward with all my strength and push him past the line he defended.

I hoped my next opponent would be as easy.

It turned out that my EIGHTMILE and sandlot reputation preceded me to the tryouts. What happened to my first opponent? He opted to drop out of the challenge for cornerback, and pursued the safety position. That day, I performed as advertised, and I earned the cornerback position. We had a few weeks to practice before the first game, and Coach held position challenges every Monday, but no one challenged me for my defensive position.

The rules of our junior high school games were a bit different than those on the high school or college levels. We didn't kickoff. We punted. When the season started, I was one of the starting cornerbacks, and the backup punt returner—I was proving my mettle as an all-around player.

Our season started out with a good news, bad news situation—we lost the first two games by a few points each, but we played pretty well. The offense was led by a little white kid, Carlton, at quarterback, and Michael at running back. If there were a weakness, it was the inability of our offense to score points—our defense was solid.

Carlton and I became good friends that year. In fact, all the blacks accepted him, thinking he was a cool guy. As the season continued, he constantly tried to convince me to challenge for an offensive position—but the only position I was interested in was running back, and Michael was the starter at that position. I just couldn't bring myself to challenge him. But, by the time we played our third game, fate came into play. We were playing Palmer Pillans Junior High, and we were down 12-0 in the second half. Suddenly, our starting punt returner was injured and had to leave the game. Coach Perry, our defense and special teams coach, called my name the next time Palmer punted—I ran onto the field, and took my position to receive the punt.

I was nervous, but I caught the ball cleanly and took off sprinting toward the strong side of the field. Suddenly, my football instincts kicked in, and I made a move reversing course to the opposite side of the field, causing some confusion for the kicking team. After several missed tackles, they brought me down a few yards short of the endzone. I trotted off the field and our offense took over, pushing the ball the last few yards for a touchdown.

The next time Palmer punted, I did the same thing. That time, I scored. Unfortunately, we lost that game as well as the one after that, but I became the starting punt returner, as well as the backup running back. Michael continued to hold down the starting running back position, while I learned all the offensive plays at practice so I would be ready to go, if needed.

We played all of our games on weekdays, so my mother couldn't attend because of her work schedule. By that time, she was only working one job at the Mobile Airport. But, the airport was too far away for her to drive to my games after work and get there before they ended. It was okay with me because I looked forward to telling her everything that happened over dinner at home—she always wanted to know every detail.

Our next game was at home against Sidney Phillips Junior High, so all the students from my school were there. We played on a field right behind the school, and the students came to our home games. I really enjoyed making a play that got the crowd excited and, during the course of the game, I returned a few punts and ran an interception to the ten-yard line. Then, to my surprise, Coach put me in the game at running back! I did pretty well, scoring our only touchdown, but we lost a hard-fought game by two points. The difference in the score was Sidney Phillips's safety when they tackled Carlton in the endzone.

The final score was 8-6.

****

As the season progressed, my classmates and the student body were promoting me as the team MVP. At this time, we had a 0-2 record with only four games left in the season. But, my luck was about to change for the worse. 'The Boys,' my new crew, were running a racket at school, and I was part of it. We met in the morning before class, planning to steal alcohol from the grocery store located on the same block as our school. From there, we brought it to school and sold it to other kids. We used the money we pocketed to buy sweatshirts as well as the lettering we put on them. We also sold an alcoholic drink called Mad Dog 20/20 that came in an assortment of flavors, and was popular with the teens. That is until one of our sales guys sold a bottle of the good stuff to a guy who couldn't keep quiet—until then, things were progressing smoothly. But, as they say, *one bad apple spoils the whole barrel*—so when the guy who bought the good stuff got busted, he spilled his guts. The school staff searched our lockers and, fortunately for me, my locker was clean. Some of the other guys weren't so lucky.

But, I didn't get off without embarrassment. The search squad found a letter from my girlfriend in my locker. The principal and guidance counselor were familiar with me because of my penchant for being sent to the principal's office quite a few times, and the principal couldn't believe my girlfriend was mixed up with me. After all, she was a good student and a popular athlete. So, he called her to his office, questioning her about our relationship. She admitted she wrote the letter, and he promptly he told her to stay away from me because I was trouble.

I was next. He called me on the carpet, and decided to suspend me despite the only evidence he had against me was the word of the boy who was busted. I thought the suspension was too harsh—it lasted through our next scheduled football game. Oh, I wasn't alone—some of my peers agreed with me. They circulated a petition to cancel the suspension, thereby allowing me to play. The principal agreed to consider it after learning many of my team members and fellow students signed it. But, it didn't take him long to deny the petition and follow through with the suspension. He called my mother at work, and informed her of the bad news.

I knew I would have to face her, so the thought crossed my mind to never go home again—I would rather be homeless than face the wrath of Betty Williams! Although my mother visited the school on several occasions due to my bad behavior, it was the first time I was suspended from school.

The bus ride home from school was the longest trip in my entire life. All I could think about was how my mother was going to react. I also knew, my sister would be there, gloating.

She would have the phone all to herself.

When I arrived, my mother wasn't there yet—but, she would make it home soon enough! The second she got home, I plead my innocence, explaining my conspiracy theory to her. She wasn't having any part of it. According to her, just because I wasn't caught in the act didn't excuse my actions (this was the first time I was accused of any type of conspiracy, and punished because a snitch told on me.) Sadly, it was a life lesson I failed to learn, and it would come back later to haunt me.

My mother wasn't the type to let me off without some sort of punishment, so there would be no phone, no playing outside, and no friends coming over. She also gave me a good whipping. To add insult to injury, she handed me a bag of ten to fifteen bottles of alcohol, and told me to drink every drop of them. Of course, she knew I couldn't handle that, but she made her point!

When I returned to school after the suspension, the sixth game of the season was already played. Not only were we soundly defeated, but Michael suffered an injury in the game. That meant I would play offense and defense for our final game. It was the first season I played cornerback, and I enjoyed the position—but I was looking forward to starting at running back, as well. The final game was against Scarborough Junior High, and we needed to win to make our season respectable.

Maybe the suspension was just what I needed, or maybe it was just blind luck that Michael got injured. But, whatever the reason, I had the best game of my young football career against Scarborough. On offense and special teams, I scored two touchdowns, one punt return, and one first down from scrimmage. On defense, I caused a fumble to set up the game-winning touchdown. It was a great feeling to win our first and only game of the season!

After my performance, I was sure I was the front runner for the MVP award, so I looked forward to the awards banquet until Coach pulled me aside. He told me I was disqualified to receive any awards as a consequence of my school suspension. I was disappointed, but it worked out okay—the MVP award went to my good friend, Carlton.

By then, I was one of the most popular guys in school. Randal was a good basketball player, and we developed our games in my mother's backyard. So, when I told him I was going to try out for the team, he decided to join me. Randal was much taller than I, but he was heavy. Nevertheless, that boy could run! He was faster than I for most of our childhood, and his physical makeup suited him for basketball. I tried to talk him into playing organized football for years, but his mother wouldn't let him. She was overprotective and didn't want to see her little boy possibly injured. So, I was surprised when she agreed to allow him try out for the basketball team. On the other hand, my mother didn't worry about injury, but once again told me in no uncertain terms, "Just like football, you can play basketball as long as your grades don't suffer."

When I showed up at the tryouts, I discovered our basketball coach was Coach Marshall from the football team. This was my first experience playing organized basketball, and I thought the tryouts were fun. Randal and I made the final cut—Randal as a power forward, and I made it as a guard. I was an average basketball player, but a good athlete which allowed me to overcome some of my height disadvantage. It turned out that our boys' basketball team was very good—but, like football, we lost more than we wanted. Even so, I continued to improve my play—I developed a decent jump shot, improved my dribbling skills and, near the end of the season, I became the starting shooting guard.

It wasn't enough.

I decided I didn't have a passion for the game. It was obvious to me basketball was a tall guy's game, and I consistently stayed small for my age. I couldn't even foresee myself reaching six feet! So, I played the game to pass the time, and for pure entertainment.

****

Blount High School was terrible in football, but dominated in basketball. Every year during Christmas break, they host a basketball tournament featuring the hottest teams in the city. The list included Le Flore, Vigor, Blount, Murphy, and Williamson—all predominantly black schools. The gym would rock with black kids from all over Mobile County, and it was the next best thing to a fashion show. Since it usually began three days after Christmas, everyone dressed up in new clothes they got for Christmas.

The 1986 tournament was the first one I attended.

I went with Marcus, king of dollar joints and nickel bags, who hustled for his older brother. Thunderbird wine was the premium drink of choice for underage drinkers, and Mitchell stopped to pick up a fat-necked bottle. He knew I wasn't green because he saw me smoke cigarettes and drink beer, so when a friend asked me to go with him to the tournament, I was jazzed—when I asked him what to wear, he told me to put on my 'fly' clothes. Fortunately, my mother bought me a nice pair of Levi's, some polo shirts, and a pair of white high-topped Reeboks for Christmas.

Finally the day came and I was dressed up, ready to go. Mom was at work, and my sister was happy to get rid of me because she wanted to spend time alone at the house. We took a shortcut, hit the road, and Mitchell had his bottle of Thunderbird with him plus a bag full of dollar joints. I thought he had way too many joints, and he told me he planned to sell 100 to 200 at the Christmas break basketball tournament. Judging by the size of the crowd when we arrived, he could accomplish his goal.

The crowd was thick, and midway through the tournament, a fight broke out. Everybody ran wild, and I stayed as close to Mitchell as possible. But when we made it outside the gym, we heard gunshots—it seemed as if an all-out war were taking place. Mitchell and I ran away from the crowd to leave the school, and while we were leaving the school grounds Mitchell stopped to retrieved his wine in the bushes where he hid it. Although I wasn't a wine drinker, I decided to drink a little—he was cool with the idea, and decided we were far enough away from the chaos to smoke the leftover joint he discovered in his pocket. I sipped the Thunderbird from the bottle, and Mitchell asked me if I wanted to smoke a joint. I had no idea what to expect, but I agreed and he warned me it wasn't like those little cigarettes I smoked. Too late. I took a hit, and began coughing uncontrollably. He laughed and said, "Next time, take it easy."

I did.

We continued our walk home, and I hallucinated a bit.

"Do you see that goat?"

No goat.

That was my first experience with pot, and Mitchell teased me about the goat for months thereafter!

****

Springtime approached rapidly, and it was time for track season. When track started again, I was the seasoned veteran with one years' experience under my belt, so I thought I should give it a try. Coach Johnson was still our track coach, and I guess he was coaching for the extra money because he really didn't have knowledge or passion for various events. His primary job was teaching science, and I used to cut up when I was in his class. In fact, one day he told me to get up in front of the class and tell jokes. Looking back, I know he was definitely trying to embarrass me in front of my classmates, but I actually enjoyed having the stage and being a clown—telling jokes and making the whole class laugh was right up my alley. So, what could've been a disaster for me ended up being a fun day. I didn't realize it then, but I know now Coach Johnson had my best interest at heart. He saw potential in me, and didn't want my unacceptable behavior to get in the way. In fact, he used to call my mother frequently to update her on my behavior issues in an attempt to keep me on the right path.

I found sprinting was a lot different than long jumping, and I wasn't the fastest sprinter on my team—just fast enough to qualify as a member of the 4 x 100 meter relay team. So, I was officially an event athlete—long jump and sprints. But, truth was I always looked forward to the end of the track season because I could turn my focus to football.

I was born to play.

Chapter 5
Sports vs. Education

Ligh school! How can a kid really know what to expect after completing grade school and junior high? Just as a high schooler doesn't have a clue what it means to be an adult, junior high schoolers are really in for surprise as they start their freshman year. For me, high school always seemed to be my highest goal in life—as if the high school I attended would predetermine the rest of my life.

I always looked forward to the day I would attend Vigor High School. Unfortunately, what was a lifelong dream turned into a nightmare when I entered the early enrollment process. Since my siblings attended Vigor High, I looked forward to continuing the family tradition. I expected my transition to high school to be as smooth as my previous transition to K. J. Clark Junior High School. I already knew a number of staff and teachers who worked there when my siblings attended—but, when I tried to complete early enrollment, I found my home address was zoned for Blount High School. How could that be?

Blount was the only other high school in Prichard, and it wasn't my school of choice, so you can imagine my disappointment when I discovered my siblings used my grandmother's address in Happy Hill Project as their home address. Doing so allowed them to enroll in Vigor High— unfortunately, I wasn't so lucky. My grandmother moved to Toulminville, and that didn't help me at all. I didn't want to go because Blount's reputation wasn't good—the campus was run down, and it had the worst football team in the county. I heard stories about it, and I also had a first-hand negative experience of my own. The year before, the starting quarterback was stabbed in the school hallway by his girlfriend—and, over Christmas break, I was lucky I wasn't shot and killed attending the annual school basketball tournament!

Our guidance counselor passed out the high school enrollment forms, and he gave me one for Blount, but I told him I wasn't going to fill it out because I was going to Vigor. When I requested the Vigor form, he explained he couldn't give me one, and advised me to request a transfer from the school board because my home was zoned for Blount. Then he suggested I go ahead and fill out the Blount form to ensure I would have a class schedule if and when I transferred. Even though I was dead set against going to Blount, I filled out the enrollment form. I learned later that K. J. Clark Junior High was split into two zones—the school itself was located in Chickasaw, Alabama, but it filtered students to three different high schools—Vigor, Blount, and Satsuma.

Some kids I associated with at Clark were zoned for Blount, but most were zoned for Vigor including my good friends. I was adamant I would attend Vigor, too, and I vowed to follow in my brother's footsteps!

Besides friends, another factor I considered was each school's athletic program. I wanted to play football with my friends, and Vigor was known for winning. Blount was known for losing. I felt strongly that attending Vigor was my best shot to achieve my goals on the football team—so, I assessed my options, and concluded I would go anywhere but Blount!

During the summer leading up to high school, I petitioned the Board of Education to attend Vigor, but the odds were against me because everyone in my mother's neighborhood was zoned for Blount. All of Randal's older siblings attended Blount, and he would be going there, as well. Leon headed to Blount. Two grades ahead of us, Randal's older brother and Leon's older brother were already attending Blount, an they were involved in the sports program—Joe played on the basketball team, and John played in the band. In my opinion, the two best things Blount had going for it were basketball and band. When I thought about it, not only had my mother and father attended Blount, I had two relatives who attended Blount the year before. Still, in my mind, there was only one bright spot for Blount.

Kandy.

Over the summer, she became my girlfriend and she was going to Blount in the fall. So, many factors came into play, yet I still hoped to attend Vigor in the fall. In fact, I blocked out reality and lived in a fantasy world by telling my friends I was going to Vigor—unfortunately, the reality was Vigor wasn't an option. When Kandy tried to convince me I should go to Blount with her, I upset her by badmouthing the school. Even my friends in her neighborhood tried to talk me into going to Blount because they wanted me to play for the football team, but I just couldn't see it. Even after I received word my petition for transfer was denied, the denial only increased my determination to go to Vigor.

Enter creativity. It was all I had left, so I looked into the requirements for a hardship transfer. One of the requirements was based on race and, as an African-American student, I qualified for transfer to any school having a black student population of less than five percent. After researching the possibilities, I discovered Baker High School was located near the Mobile Airport where my mother worked. The student population of Baker was over ninety-five percent white, but I didn't know anyone who went there. When I discussed it with Mom, she said if that's what I wanted, I should go for it.

Having her support, I submitted a transfer request for Baker, but it was also denied. Up until then, I was still preparing to attend Vigor, and even started lifting weights to increase my strength before the start of football season. After my second transfer was denied, reality finally hit home and I realized—barring a fake address—I would be attending Blount.

My weight conditioning started with Michael and his crew. Since one of his weightlifting buddies was already a Vigor student, they used the weight room at the school. Michael's specialty was the bench press, and he competed with the older, bigger guys. He and the others were out of my league, so I stayed away from the school, and only lifted in the backyard. Although I couldn't compete in the weight room, I was well respected as a serious football player around the Prichard area. While playing for Clark, I exhibited a high skill level, as well as a keen knowledge of the game. Unfortunately, I still had my dark side—hanging around, drinking, and smoking on occasion, furthering my gang mentality.

Around that time, I met a guy named Jimmy Kirkwood who lived in Michael's neighborhood. He was a good athlete, owning the reputation as a beast in the neighborhood pickup games and, as a senior at Blount, he made a name for himself playing basketball and football. That's not all— he was the best player on Blount's football team, as well as team captain. Jimmy thought I would attend Vigor because my siblings did, and he told me several times he liked my game. He also said when the word got out I was going to be a Blount student in the fall, he was ecstatic—he wanted me to try out for the varsity team.

As summer progressed, stress took over. I was just shy of my fourteenth birthday, and I never set foot inside a high school classroom—the last thing I expected was attending the Blount varsity football team tryouts prior to the start of school. Again, I discussed it with Mom and, as usual, she didn't have any problem with my trying out. The only concern was I pass a physical exam and had insurance, so the official paperwork was submitted. I showed up at the tryouts with Jimmy, and he introduced me to all the coaches. Coach Gamble was a short man with the Jerry curl, and he had a goal to win—unfortunately, the only thing listed on his coaching résumé was a string of bad seasons.

The first day of tryouts was a meet and greet, and I spent most of my time meeting the players. I couldn't help noticing some of the eighteen to nineteen year old players had full-grown beards, and it was apparent I would be one of the youngest and smallest players on the field. I officially measured at 5'6", and 145 pounds, but, much to my surprise, a young man smaller than I showed up to join us. A starter, he was the second best player on the team—5'5" and 155 pounds with amazing quickness. And, he had football skills. He was also a member of the group known as The Smurfs, and there was one member of the group who took a liking to me—Ty Gold.

Ty was a junior returning after his starting season as a defensive back. He was a good player and respected by his teammates, but defensive back was a position I decided I wanted. Turned out I wouldn't compete with Ty because he defended the right side of the field, and I hoped to win the same position on the left side. I was confident, but I was also aware I was still young compared to the guys with whom I would be competing.

I quickly learned I wasn't the only freshman trying out, but I was the youngest and the smallest. The other freshman trying out that year were Jackson Pruitt, Jason Black, and Big Jack. I met Big Jack in Kandy's neighborhood, and he was the biggest guy on the entire team even though he was only a freshman.

All of us made the team.

Over the summer, I improved my strength, but I didn't have Ty's skills. Thankfully, he took me under his wing and taught me how to play the position. It's the same today as it was then—there is no substitute for a good mentor and coach, and Ty helped me to develop an excellent tackling technique. Things were looking good! Big Jack, Jason, and I became starters although I only played on special teams. To top it off, at the end of summer practice The Smurfs voted me in as a member of their group.

I did well in practices, and my teammates liked the way I played. Nonetheless, they thought I needed to gain strength, as well as put in more work on the fundamentals of my position—it wasn't until the first game their message started to sink in. The game was on the first Friday after the first week of school, and I thought it was cool because we were allowed to wear our team jerseys to school on game day. The only negative was since I was a freshman, no one knew me.

Blount was a crazy school—I did okay socially, but I was having problems in the classroom. It took time to get used to a school where the walls were painted with graffiti —not by vandals, but by amateur graffiti artists. Pipes hung from the hallway ceilings, and students were somewhat out of control, hanging around the corridors outside of their classrooms all day long. My opinion? Blount was the spitting image of the Morgan Freeman movie, *Lean on Me*. The school tipped to a low point on the academic scale, and it seemed as if the teachers didn't care at all. I think it may have been the poorest high school in the Mobile public school system—but, in a weird way, all the negatives made the school fun to attend, and my past behavior problems allowed me to blend right in.

Surprisingly, I enjoyed my initial experience at Blount. It didn't take long to get into the swing of things with all the activities going on, one of which was the Friday pep rally prior to the football games. Pep rallies were new to me, but they were definitely the social event of the week. The rallies took place at the gym, and everyone at the school attended, purple and white gold accented school colors on display everywhere! Students were divided by class, and each class had its own seating section. The varsity football team sat on a stage, the band played songs, and cheerleaders were leading cheers. Sitting up there on the stage with the team made me feel special, and it was a good feeling to know all the students supported us.

Everything was a learning experience, and it surprised me to find out some of the older players left school to get high before the pep rallies. I was never quite sure if the coaches tolerated it, or they weren't aware of what was going on. Still . . .

I was only one of four freshmen on the varsity football team, and I wore jersey #41 which was the same number my brother wore at Vigor. As it worked out, I tended to hang around with the older guys on the team, and it seemed as if I were constantly looking for an older male role model. Some kids grow up faster than others, and although I was a very young freshman, I already gained life experience. I was sexually active, drank alcohol, smoked cigarettes, and was introduced to drugs in the form of marijuana. What else was there for me to do?

Sometime during the football season, I took an aptitude test and scored well. I never considered myself smart, but my scores qualified me for the gifted student program. I'm not sure how it happened, but the school convinced me to sign up for advanced placement classes and, to this day, I don't know why I agreed. I wasn't into the classwork, and I had a social life—AP took up a lot of my time! To me, AP classes were for nerds, and it was a big mistake for me to be involved. However, after I discussed the situation with my mother, she thought I should give it a try. I'm sure she was happy and proud of me, so I agreed to try it for the first quarter.

As time went on, I started to hang out with Ty a lot. We had a great deal in common, and both of us played as youth league players at EIGHTMILE. Even better, we were members of The Smurfs. We enjoyed partying and had girlfriends—not sure, but maybe that's why we only won one game the entire season . . .

After winning our first game 7-6, we lost all the rest of our games by at least thirty points each. Ty sustained an unexpected season-ending injury in the first game, and I thought Coach would put me in his position. But, our defense coach, Coach Adams, had other ideas. He was a chain-smoking, black, old man. Apparently, he didn't think I could handle the responsibility of Ty's position, so he didn't play me. Even when we were behind by thirty points in the fourth quarter, Coach Adams wouldn't look my way. Instead, he played Jimmy Collins both ways—offense and defense. At halftime of each game, Jimmy approached Coach Adams to tell him to play me in his place during the third and fourth quarters, but he never did. All I ever played was special teams, most likely because I was one of the smallest guys on the team.

Blount had a varsity and freshman football team, but the freshman team didn't start its season until after school started. All the freshman who didn't make the varsity team in the summer could play on that team and, although I made the varsity team, Coach Campbell wanted me to play on the freshman team, as well—I was the only varsity freshman allowed to do so. Our freshman coach was Coach Michaels, and, as it turned out, we only had a total of eleven players. Our first game was against the Vigor freshman, and I played offensive guard. Although we started the game with eleven players, our quarterback got hurt so Coach Michaels ordered me onto the field.

Vigor's student population was larger than Blount's, and their football programs were ahead of ours. A bunch of my friends were on the Vigor freshman team, and it was fun to play against them. However, since I didn't know any of my team's plays, all I did was snap the ball and run. We lost the game 6-0, but it was a great morale booster for Blount. We hung in there against a strong football program, and played them evenly for almost the entire second half. With only ten players! It was great to have a few of the varsity guys come out to support us and, soon after, word got around about what we accomplished in our first game. Our success encouraged some of the other freshmen to join the team and, since we needed all the help we could get, it was motivating. Because I felt good about the freshman team, I tried to convince Randal to play with us, but, his mother still wouldn't give him permission to play—she was still worried about his getting injured although he was one of the biggest boys in the ninth grade. Not as big as Big Jack, but still big.

Our success in the first game paid dividends, and we wound up with sixteen players. More players gave us more options, but it still meant many of us would have to play both ways. Coach Michaels decided to leave me at quarterback, and also assigned me to one of the defensive cornerback positions. It was the best of both worlds for me—I loved playing defense, and I would gain experience playing offense. I was small and quick, and learned to tackle well, but strength still wasn't one of my assets. To be successful at the varsity level, I knew I had to be stronger, and making a commitment to lifting weights was the only option to earn a starting varsity position.

Lifting weights. Again.

After our 6-0 loss to Vigor, we went on a tear. Playing sandlot games, I learned to pass the ball fairly well and, although passing wasn't my strongest attribute, I quickly learned I was a much better running quarterback than passer. Nimble with exceptional balance, I possessed a natural gift making me hard to tackle and, when I ran the ball, it was rare the first man would get his hands on me.

We had three good freshmen players on the varsity, but Coach Campbell wouldn't allow them to play with us— it was disappointing, and I imagined how good our team would be with three additional guys. Even with our limited roster, we won games by an average of forty points—stark contrast to the team that lost every game by an average of over thirty points. It wasn't unusual for me to run for three or four touchdowns, as well as pass for three or four touchdowns in the same game. With that kind of success, I earned the nickname of 'The Magician' by mid-season— you might say I was the Houdini of Blount High's freshman team!

Whenever we had a home game, the varsity players watched us play after practice—finally recognizing us as well as the rest of the student body—and they began to support us. I think we were the first Blount football team to have a winning season in a long time, and it wasn't too long before students joked that the freshman team should play our varsity games on Friday nights. Of course, I was already the lone member of the freshman team who was also playing varsity, although I only played on kickoffs.

As the season continued, some of my varsity teammates tried to convince the coach to play me more. Their efforts increased after they watched me play in a couple of my freshmen games, but Coach Campbell had his favorite saying—*you don't pour no wine before its time.*

Playing more wasn't to be.

Our freshman team became a closely-knit group. We hung out, and we liked the feeling winning gave us—but, there was also a down side. Some of the guys wanted to be on the varsity team because I was on it, wear their jerseys to school on game day, and be on stage during the pep rallies. To them, it didn't matter if they played one down of football as long as they could be a part of the team activities. I understood their feelings, but I felt differently— wearing a jersey to school or being on stage in a pep rally was secondary to me. My focus was to be on the field. I remember one of my freshmen teammates always asked

Coach Campbell if he could be on the varsity team. Coach turned him down again and again, but for some reason Coach made me stay. At one point, I convinced myself I wanted to get off the varsity team. Our varsity team sucked, and it was an embarrassing situation to get blown off the field week after week. I stood on the sidelines feeling as if there were nothing I could do to prevent them from losing. Even so, the strongest reason for my wanting off the team was all my freshmen teammates would be in the stands, wearing freshman jerseys, and hanging out together at the Friday night games. While I stood on the sidelines watching a losing effort, it seemed they were having much more fun—everyone recognized the freshman team in the stands, and ignored the varsity game. I knew the guys would be bragging about being winners, and telling stories about how they played in the game that week. I wanted to be part of that, and I also wanted to hang out with Kandy.

There comes a point in life, young or old, when you realize it doesn't matter what you want. You just have to play the hand dealt to you. Coach Campbell—having none of my grief—told me, "If you don't stay on the varsity team, you won't be allowed to participate on the freshman team." That was it. I had no choice but to stay on the varsity team. At first I was upset, but then I realized every cloud has a silver lining, and Blount High School's silver lining was their band. Although we were getting blown out at every home game, the crowd packed the stands for the halftime show.

Instead of watching the band perform at halftime, I went to the locker room with my team while my freshmen teammates rocked with the band—I was a big part of why the spotlight was on them, but all I could do was suck it up and live with it.

The freshman season was shorter than the varsity season, and it finally came to an end. My team finished with a 5-1 record, and I had a great year. Since the varsity still had a few games remaining, some of the more talented freshmen were allowed to dress with us for remaining home games. During the last game of the season, Coach Campbell finally put me in—I guess he figured we were so far behind that any play I made would be insignificant. But, you know by now it wasn't like me to waste an opportunity. For the final drive of the game as well as the final game of the season I played quarterback, driving my team the length of the field, capping off the drive for a touchdown pass to Jimmy Collins in the corner of the endzone. It was an amazing feeling, and an amazing way to end my first season of football at Blount!

At season's end, Kandy and I were still a couple, although things grew rocky during the season. She resented my hanging out with the upperclassman as well as attending their parties with Ty. She also found out I was spending time talking to some of the older girls, one in particular. The girl was attractive, and some would've called my approaching her social suicide. So, we talked on occasion, and she never showed any real interest in me. I guess I could've felt rejected, but I wasn't offended. It wasn't the first time, and I was sure it wouldn't be the last. As a result, Kandy began to mix with the older crowd and, although our relationship survived football season, we agreed to part ways soon after. Yes, it was bummer, but I was spending more time on athletics, and it was for the best.

At the end of the football season, Coach called us together, explaining it was mandatory for us to participate in a minimum of two sports—if we wanted to do more, we could. Playing two sports didn't bother me, but that was about to change when first quarter grades came out. During the season, I concentrated on football and neglected my classes and, when I received my grades, I didn't even have one 'A' on my report card. I failed one class for the first time in my life. That failing grade meant I had to drop out of the AP program and return to taking regular classes. Worse, my mother was true to her word, and it was the end of my participation in sports, as well. Education was important in my family, and Mom was serious about it. If we were going to go to college, we had to graduate from high school—dropping out of school was never an option. When my mother saw my first quarter grades, she had a fit and demanded an explanation. She wasn't aware I was having academic or behavior issues—unlike Clark, Blount teachers didn't contact parents to discuss behavior problems. That said, I believe the teachers at Blount were so overwhelmed and frustrated by the large amount of problems that occurred at school every day, they felt hopeless. Over the years, they must have concluded it was a waste of time to ask parents to intervene. Truth was things were out of control, and I believe eighty percent of the students had behavior problems.

Being kicked out of the gifted program didn't bother me because I thought sports were more important than getting a high-quality education. Yes, I had ambitions of going to college, but as a young freshman I didn't make the connection between academic performance and college entrance. Besides, my mother was clear if my grades suffered, sports were out. So, until then, I didn't pay attention to college football—I was more focused on high school rather than professional games. But, I was aware some of the guys who played at Blount went on to play for the University of Alabama, as well as Auburn University. They returned to our school occasionally to speak to student athletes about their universities and sports programs, and I heard various players in our state were superstars at the schools—names such as Bo Jackson, Keith McCants, and Cornelius Bennett. It's ironic I didn't have any interest in the University of Alabama—that year, I became an LSU fan mainly because I liked their colors.

They were the same as Blount's.

The word in my hood was the University of Alabama was a racist white school that hated blacks. Back in the 1960s, Governor George Wallace stood at the school entrance and refused to allow the first black student to enter. Ever since I heard that story, I had a strong dislike for the university. And, when my mother learned of my interest in attending LSU, she started to purchase a lot of different LSU paraphernalia—sweatshirts, T-shirts, and whatever else she could find. It seemed as if she liked the idea, so I began to set my sights on attending the school.

In addition to Blount graduates who attended universities in the State of Alabama, there was one was attending LSU—James Evans. James had a nephew named Lamont who was one year older than I, and he also attended Blount. Since Lamont and I were good friends and varsity teammates, I felt I had a direct connection to LSU. After listening to what the guys had to say about their school admission requirements, as well as receiving a wake-up call for my first quarter grades, I realized I needed to take classes and earn grades that were appropriate to qualify me for college. The courses weren't the basic or general high school courses, but they weren't the advanced program courses, either.

Another wake-up call—I wasn't allowed to try out for the basketball team. I learned if my mother said I could play a high school sport, it didn't mean I could play. Fortunately for me, I didn't completely rebel and my grades improved for the second quarter. By spring, my grades were much better, and I was again eligible to play sports and compete. I had my choice of baseball, or track and field. Track was familiar to me, having competed at Clark, but I never played any kind of organized baseball. All I knew about baseball was by pickup softball games at church picnics, family reunions, and in the neighborhood. I knew the basic rules, but had zero playing experience—nevertheless, I decided to give it a try.

Each sport at Blount offered two levels—freshman, and varsity. A few of the guys from football also played baseball, not because they liked to, but to satisfy Coach Gamble's rule requiring all of us to participate in two sports. I tried out for the freshman team, and Coach decided to play me at second base. I really wasn't more than an average player, but my athleticism got me by. I wasn't enthusiastic about playing, but it was cool because a few of the guys from my freshman football team joined me during tryouts. I was even less excited when I found out the first game was going to be against Mary Montgomery High School.

Mary Montgomery was one of the schools known for their baseball program. Their entire team was white, while our team was all black, and we were thrown together, resembling the Bad News Bears. They, on the other hand, looked like a bunch of pros. No surprise. We lost!

So much for my baseball career.

Track and field tryouts began that same week and what I liked most about track was it was coed, while football and baseball were strictly for boys. At Blount, the girls and boys track team practiced and traveled together and, although I thrived on sports competition, I also liked hanging around the girls. Best of both worlds! Time passed since my breakup with Kandy, and I started to develop an interest in a few different girls. One in particular, Marilyn Smith, caught my eye. We were in the same grade, and she was the quiet type who tended to stay to herself—she was also pretty with a cute smile. Since we didn't have any classes together, I had to look for her and, when I saw her at school, I flirted. She didn't have a boyfriend, and she was obviously shy—she'd never had a boyfriend before.

Marilyn lived with her father and mother in the Bessemer Projects just five minutes from my house—she was the oldest of three children with two younger brothers. I found out she hung out with a group of girls who were known to be somewhat promiscuous, and that seemed odd, because she was so shy. I knew a guy on my freshman track team who was dating one of the girls in her social circles, so one day I happened to be at his house when Marilyn and her girlfriends came over. She and I started talking, and we hit it off instantly.

That day she became my girlfriend.

****

The track season was successful and fun, and our team was one of the best in the city. We had a few fast guys on varsity and freshman teams and, that year, Jason Black was a freshman but he was brought up to varsity to run. He became a part of a relay team that set a record for the State of Alabama.

Early in the season, I started out competing in field events. It was my first year as a triple jumper, and when it came to field events we had some talented boys who excelled by their natural ability. I was a natural triple jumper, learning how to compete in the event by watching my brother when he was in high school. Since my sprint speed improved, I earned a leg up on the freshman's 4 x 100 relay team. My track coach was an old-school type named Coach Terry, and he was known to the team as 'Tiptoe Terry.' He coached the sport for twenty years, earning his nickname by consistently demonstrating how sprinters should always be running on their toes. His favorite events were the sprints, but he was knowledgeable about all aspects of track and field. Coach Terry enjoyed spending time working with the sprinters, but not the distance runners for the field events. Luckily, I was a sprinter and field event participant, and I learned a lot from Tiptoe Terry. Looking back, I'm glad I ran track, because it helped me increase my speed for football.

It was unfortunate track was always viewed as a secondary sport by Coach Gamble. So, when football started in the middle of track season, being a member of the track team was no excuse to miss spring football practice. Fortunately, if a track meet occurred, we had permission to skip practice in order to compete in the meet. However, even though our varsity team wasn't much good, it still took priority over track. We anticipated a promising sophomore year with all of our freshman returning as well as the return starters from the previous year. Out of a total of seventeen freshman players, only nine reported to spring practice. By that time, the others either quit school, or lost interest in the sport. Me? My athletic endeavors were going well.

It was mandatory for all football players to take a varsity athletic class during the season, so I took that time as an opportunity to seriously start lifting weights before the summer break. I was a serious weightlifter, considerably improving my strength, and I also put on an additional five pounds of muscle mass. The result? Tackling those older and bigger boys on the field wasn't so difficult!

I looked forward to making good use of my time that summer. My grades were back up to a satisfactory level, and I seemed to fit in well at Blount. Vigor rapidly receded to a distant memory, and I was getting involved in neighborhood pickup football and basketball games. I was a Blount High School sophomore, a starting defensive cornerback on the varsity football team, and considered one of the oldest kids in the neighborhood games—even though I was still only fourteen years old.

The future was looking bright for Blount football—and, me!

Chapter 6
Learning to Win

My freshman year and the transition from junior high to senior high at Blount went reasonably well. The high school was different than I expected because I always expected to attend Vigor. But, by the time school started again in the fall, I accepted the fact there was nothing I could do to change the situation. So, I decided to make the best of it.

The previous fall, Vigor, garnered the 6A State Championship, and approached the upcoming season as the number one team in the nation. Their team was loaded with talent, but I often wondered if I attended there would I've gotten a chance to play? I was sure the special teams players at Vigor were a cut above those at Blount—but, I was now a member of the Blount varsity team, so I focused on whatever I needed to do to raise our school to the same level as Vigor. Yet, there was one thing I could never influence at that time—Blount's standing as the poorest school in the district. I knew overcoming a lack of funding was going to be the school's greatest challenge.

At the beginning of summer, there was a major rumor going around Prichard that the Board of Education was planning to close Blount High School due to its poor academic standing as well as aging facilities—both in need of repair. Apparently, the plan was to move the school to a different location, and change its name. The entire city was in an uproar over the rumored plan and current, former, and alumni students fought against the school board's taking any action. Although many thought the school was too far beyond repair, eventually the board reconsidered its plans. The new plan was to keep Blount open, and renovate the campus on its present site. In addition to upgrading the facilities, the board also decided to get rid of the school's entire administration and staff—with a few exceptions. As part of this reorganization, Coach Gamble and his staff were let go.

It was the start of a new regime for Blount High School's academics and athletics.

During the shakeup, there was a reassessment of the current athletic standing of the school relative to other high schools in the area. Since the school's legal ranking was based on the size of the student body, it insured small schools were not forced to unfairly compete with large schools in any athletic endeavors. The reassessment resulted in Blount's reclassification from 6A to 5A based on updated and accurate student attendance. It was improperly classified as a 6A school for years due to overstatement of their student population numbers. The school ignored the low attendance caused by its high dropout rate, and the staff wasn't diligent in reporting an accurate headcount on their daily attendance sheets.

The move from 6A to 5A sparked a significant change in our upcoming football schedule. No longer would we play at the top 6A level—instead, we would match up with 5A schools of equivalent size in our region, competing for the 5A playoff spots at the end of the regular season. But, our non-league games would continue against our traditional 6A rivals such as Leflore and Vigor.

The biggest game of the regular season, perhaps the year, was still against Vigor, and it was a vintage rivalry bringing the entire town of Prichard out to watch the game. Although the outcome of the game was normally predictable, due to Vigor's vast superiority, the Blount fans still celebrated the fact their band was extremely talented. Historically, Vigor's victories came on the field—Blount's came during the halftime show.

With the good news that Blount wouldn't be closing or moving to another location, I focused on training for the upcoming season. My grades were to my mother's satisfaction, so my main focus was to get to the weight room often as well as train hard—I was eager to participate and do my part to bring Blount into the record books. Since I earned enough credits, I passed to the tenth grade, securing my eligibility to play sports during the coming year. Fortunately, my behavior problems in the classroom started to subside—but I don't think I changed my overall behavior. It seemed the teachers were more tolerant of men, and even when I acted out in some way, my teachers seemed to be all right with it—or, they didn't care enough to inform my mother. I'm not sure which.

As we moved into summer, the varsity team agreed to continue its workouts, so we met at the school at a predetermined time. I was more passionate and serious about football than at any other time in my life, and I became obsessed with strength conditioning and physical fitness. Finally, I overcame my reluctance to lift weights, and I was more goal oriented. Before Coach Gamble left, he devised a program to motivate his players to improve their strength in the weight room. The system consisted of different performance strength levels, and he created a specific club for each. In order to reward achievement, he had T-shirts and sweatshirts printed with the club name, and personalized them with our names for those of us achieving membership in a particular club. There were three clubs or categories of performance strength—bench press, squats, and dead lifts.

The lowest strength level was the 200 Pound Club, and some of the older guys reached the 400, 500, or 600 Pound Clubs. I started at the 150 pound level, and set my goal to become a member of the 200 Pound Club. My maximum lift was bench pressing 135 pounds, my squat was no better, and my dead lift was even worse. But, in spite of my dismal bench pressing, I developed exceptional ball skills, but I lacked strength compared to my peers. Funny thing was I lifted the same amount of weight as my 300-pound friend, Big Jack. We often lifted together, spotting for each other in the weight room. He obviously had considerably more potential to gain strength, and I noticed he became stronger faster than I. After one month, Big Jack reached the 200-Pound Club in both bench press and squat, and his success motivated me to work harder.

Since Big Jack and I were already good friends, he and I hung out together after workouts. His neighborhood, The Bottom, was closest to the school so I went to his house, or he would hang out at mine. And, because we were also part of last year's freshman class, we hung out with the entire group whenever we could, continuing our lasting bond. Big Jack told me the older guys on our team often drank alcohol before the games, and I confessed to drinking and smoking sometimes—but, not on a regular basis. I also told him I would never drink before a game. I couldn't imagine being able to perform on the field under the influence!

As you can imagine, there's always a sadness when childhood fades—that summer, neighborhood football games dwindled for whatever reason. Bobby moved with his family to the other side of town, Leon wasn't interested in sports anymore, and Randal's mom was still paranoid about his getting hurt playing football with us—so, he didn't play. Fortunately for him, his mother didn't feel the same way about basketball—Randal and his older brother played for the school. The result? The Prichard Stadium Bulldogs were defunct.

My only source of summer football was a few pickup games in The Bottom, so Big Jack and I actually put a small team together and challenged the other hoods in the area such as Bayshore and Grant Circle. My strategy was to play games to improve my skills, plus test my strength against new competition. Some of the boys played organized football for the park league for their school, and others considered themselves gangsters. The so-called gangsters were tough guys who toted pistols, and during one pickup game against Grant Circle there was a fight between one of our players and a guy on the Grant Circle team. Although it was common for fights to break out during games in the hood, or even during some of the old Prichard Stadium Bulldog games, this one was different.

It got personal.

After my teammate got the best of him, the Grant Circle boy left the field, returned with a gun, and started running around while shooting at my teammate. After chasing us into someone's backyard, he was intent on shooting both of us—fortunately, his gun jammed when he pulled the trigger. My teammates seized the moment, smashed him across the head, took the weapon, and pistol whipped him with his own gun. Guys in the hood brought guns to the pickup games before, and some even pulled them out to make threats. But, this was the first time I felt my life was in danger. Having literally dodged a bullet, we talked it over and there was only one solution—we needed to get guns of our own.

It's a sad statement, but one of the easiest things to find in the city of Prichard was a gun. Someone needing a gun could walk in most areas of Prichard, and bump into someone willing to sell one. The going rate was $100 for a decent one and, since I saved money from one of my old hustles, I bought a snubnosed thirty-eight. At that time, it was also popular to have a sawed-off twelve gauge shotgun, and a couple of our guys came up with those. We vowed the next time someone pulled a gun on us, we wouldn't run.

We would stand our ground.

****

Mobile is a city of open land and free space, so, we got together in an open field to set up targets and shoot guns. We practiced to get used to our weapons, and improve our aim—and, for the rest of that summer, I didn't go anywhere without my weapon. There were shots fired during the Blount Christmas basketball tournament, and now shots were fired at me during a pickup game in the hood. I felt as if my life could have been taken in both situations, and I was helpless to defend myself. Just walking the streets of Prichard wasn't safe, and it was always possible to be the victim of someone's crime. When I carried the pistol with me, I felt more powerful and in control, almost as if I were daring someone to cross the line.

That year, I became friends within Rich Robinson. He was a tall, lanky kid who played defense and safety on my freshman football team and, with such long legs, he had the stride to cover a lot of ground quickly. He also ran freshman track as a distance runner, and he was respected as a decent athlete.

Rich's family lived in the Queen's Court housing project—one with high crime areas where drugs were sold, and drug addicts cruised the streets twenty-four hours a day, hustling and purchasing drugs. A few major drug dealers lived in the project, using it as their storefront—local addicts knew where to go and who see to get their short-term fix. Whenever we hung out in the neighborhood, it was common for druggies to approach, mistaking us for dealers. It made sense, too—major dealers always used kids in the projects to work as neighborhood salesmen on street corners. Since we hung out in the project, we knew a few young boys our age who were dealing—one of them known as one of the biggest drug dealers in the area. The easy access, plus the large supply of drugs in the black community surrounding Mobile, is one of the biggest reasons for high levels of violence and poverty in the black neighborhoods.

Even with it's high drug trafficking area, Queen's Court had a grass field located in the middle of the project where we used to play small pickup football games. Rich and I joined on occasion just to pass the time and, since I was a new face in Queen's, none of the local kids knew who I was. Rich's crew was small, similar to my old crew in Prichard—boys like Randal, Bobby, and Leon. His crew had a familiar feel for me, and I liked hanging out with them. We kicked it together whenever we could, and the one thing different from my own crew was they weren't really into sports—it was the hustle of the poverty-stricken projects that brought them together.

Queen's was different from my neighborhood. It seemed as if they played football to pass time until their next hustle—they weren't into it for the love of the sport like I was. In fact, since they were hustlers, there was always an abundance of weed and alcohol available, leading me to smoke and drink more than ever before. Rich was my teammate and friend, but he was different from the guys in his crew. At that time, he wasn't a hustler, but his crew shared everything with him and, since I was his friend, they welcomed me to join in on all activities. I learned early on that most of them carried guns, and I was cool with that since I no longer felt safe without my own gun.

Although I was totally into football and other sports that summer, one of the most popular activities for kids in my hood was to go roller skating, and I learned to skate at an early age at James Skating Rink in Prichard. My sisters took me with them, and I learned the basics but wasn't good enough for any form of competition. Good thing skating was like riding a bike—once I had the skates laced up on my feet, everything I learned came back to me. But, as a teenager, the skating venue changed. No longer did we hang out at James Skating Rink—Skate World was our rink of choice.

Skate World was located outside of Prichard a little to the west, but it was still inside the Mobile city limits. Too far to walk, I rode my bike to Rich's house, met up with the rest of the guys, and rode to the rink, usually piling into a car rented from a crack head by one of the guys in our group. Or, sometimes, one of the older guys drove his own car. Either way, skating was on Wednesdays and Sundays because, on those nights, the crowd was predominantly black kids. We packed the rink, and the music was tailored for our age group and culture. Later in the evening, the rink changed moods, transforming into a roller derby format consisting of sprints, relays, and the fastest lap competitions. The winners received prizes ranging from snack coupons to free admissions, but even though I was a good skater, the competitions didn't interest me—the last hour of the evening was more to my liking. When the roller derby competition ended, all skates had to be turned in so the rink could transform into the dance floor. This was my favorite time as I was always a much better dancer than skater. It was the best time to meet up with girls from all over the Mobile metro area, and it was a great way to end the evening.

The boys in Rich's crew were good dancers, and I wasn't so bad myself. We lined up and made our way through the crowds of people on the dance floor, doing our favorite dance steps—a sure way to attract girls to join in with us. But, it also had its problems. Some of the guys from other areas of Mobile would get upset with us for attracting the girls from their side of town. They were territorial, and felt we were stealing their girls away from them—as if they owned rights to them. A few times, we had no option except to physically fight our way out of the situation. Although guns weren't allowed inside Skate World, it seemed most nights ended with fistfights of some kind. Sadly, it got to the point that our sole purpose for going to the rink was to seek revenge for the previous week. On occasion, gunfire capped off the late-night dance party and, in retrospect, I'm surprised there weren't more murders committed.

****

My priority during summer vacation was to work out and continue to prepare for the upcoming football season. Having made a commitment to a strength and physical fitness conditioning program, my strength improved and I gained a few more pounds of muscle mass. I hadn't yet met my goal of membership in the 200 Pound Club when the official news of the firing of Coach Campbell and his assistant came down. After twenty years, our varsity team would have a new head coach, and I had mixed emotions about it. It was a shock to most of the underclassmen, who seemed to have an issue with it, so they put together a petition to block the firing of our coach and his staff. What they didn't know was that the firing didn't come from the Blount administration—it came from the school board, and convincing the Board to reverse its decision was nearly impossible. I signed the petition mainly because Coach Campbell promised me more playing time the following season. Upperclassman wanted him back to ensure they kept their starting positions from the year before.

It was clear—change is never easy.

The team fought hard for Coach Campbell, but there wasn't much we could do. The board denied the petition and, by the end of the summer, the new coach was on the payroll. Many of the team members still didn't want to accept the school board's decision, so when our new coach scheduled his first practice, he called a team meeting. At the time, he had no idea a large number of my teammates planned to boycott. I told myself I rode with them throughout the petition process, but I wasn't going to boycott. Unlike the others, I committed to the meeting and the first practice—when I told Big Jack about my decision, he decided to join up with me.

By the beginning of school, the school campus was

undergoing comprehensive renovations, and we had to change up our practices to play at EIGHTMILE. On the day of our first practice, Big Jack and I showed up as well as four of our teammates who also decided to ignore the boycott. We had six players—not nearly enough guys to make up one complete offense or defense. During the meeting, the coach introduced himself and his staff—Ben Harris, and his Assistant Offensive Coordinator was Coach Parker. Coach Baggett was our Defensive Coordinator. Baggett was white, but there was another black man, Dexter Pettway, who was a firefighter, and he volunteered his time to help coach the team. Turned out Coach Harris and Coach Pettway were childhood friends while playing football for Tillman High School. Coach Harris was a tall man with a slender build, playing quarterback in college for Alabama State University. I learned he had a strong arm, bad knees, and, ironically, we discovered he was a better basketball player than football player.

Earlier that day, Coach Pettway saw a few of our absentee players in front of the school, and he tried to encourage them to come to the team meeting and first practice. They heard him out, but they had no intention of breaking the boycott the first day. Me? I didn't care because without them I was sure it guaranteed me the chance to pick any position I wanted, and I was dead set on playing cornerback.

Coach Pettway was in charge of the defensive secondary so, by my earning the position, he would be my primary coach. Tank Brown was in charge of the offensive line, and William Carpenter watched over the defensive line—they worked with Big Jack and the other guys. Since our starting quarterback from the previous season was part of the boycott, Coach Harris threw all of our passes on that first day of practice. He quickly noticed how well I caught the ball, so he insisted I play wide receiver. I never played the position before—still, I learned when I was young boy. I told Coach Harris I previously played running back in the park league and during junior high school. I also reminded him I played QB for Blount's freshman team the year before. I explained my current interest and passion was for defense, and I was there to try out for cornerback. Offense was fun, but I was a defensive player at heart, and Coach Pettway already decided he wanted me to play on the defense. Since we only had six players that day, Coach Harris and Coach Pettway agreed to list me at both positions on the roster—wide receiver, and cornerback. Several days later, some of the other players decided to give up on the boycott, and join up with our team. When they returned, I already had those two starting positions locked up—last year's starters for those positions graduated, and the other players couldn't make a claim on them. They made their choice to voluntarily miss the first practice, and they had to live with the consequences.

Our starting QB returned for his senior season. He was a tall guy, and he seemed to fit Coach Harris's vision for the position. We were still missing some of the players from my freshman team, and I found out why—some were still boycotting while others had failed to achieve the grades necessary to keep them eligible to play. Unfortunately, two of the ineligible players were Rich Robinson and Ben Martin, good friends of mine.

By the end of the summer, we put together a pretty good varsity team. A good number of our starting players from the previous year returned, and we added some of our freshman team into the mix. In my mind, it was enough to make a difference, and Blount was finally looking like a team that had potential to win some games!

Dropping down from 6A to 5A was a big benefit. We didn't have the depth to compete at the higher level, and while we carried a total of twenty-five to thirty active players, the average 6A school would have fifty to sixty active players on the same team. In fact, a powerhouse school like Vigor had seventy to eighty active varsity players, and there was no way we could compete with any of these schools for a full four quarters of football. Going into my sophomore year, it was obvious some of us on the varsity football team were forced to play both ways, offense and defense. Even though we didn't have enough quality players to fill two separate lineups, I had experience from my freshman team since Big Jack and I played both sides of the ball. For our first year, I started at cornerback and wide receiver for most of the season.

****

The class of '89 was an athletic and talented group of players. Ty Gold and our QB were part of this elite group, and our class of '91 added a few more. It was exciting to start the season as the first step toward establishing a winning tradition—most of our upperclassman weren't winners at Blount while playing for Coach Campbell, and the team seemed to sense things would be different under Coach Harris. But I didn't think of it that way—I was on a team that won the EIGHTMILE park league championship, and my freshman team had a winning season the previous year. Yet, there were a lot of unknowns ahead—I wasn't convinced that year's team believed in itself, but I knew we had a good coach, staff, and raw talent. In fact, I believed so strongly in our team that I thought if Blount varsity football were ever going to have a winning season, that was it!

Our first game of the season was against Atmore High School. By that time, we knew Coach Harris hated to lose because he was passionate about winning, and it didn't matter if he were playing a game of marbles. But, even though we fought hard, we lost our first game on the road. A rumor spread quickly throughout the school that after the game Coach Harris cried on the bus ride home. Losing wasn't exactly a new experience to me, but I shared Coach Harris's passion for winning. After we lost to Atmore, my mind took me back to one of our losses when I was playing in the EIGHTMILE park league—I'll always remember crying after that loss. I gave it my all, and my emotions took hold.

Sometimes, a loss is more valuable than a win, and after we lost our first game it seemed as if a light came on—every member of our team came together with one common goal. Although I didn't realize it at the time, it seemed Coach Harris's passion for winning was contagious.

From that day forward, winning was the only option.

****

No doubt about it—history was in the making! We ticked off five straight victories in a row, changing the spirit of our school. The students of Blount High School had newly refurbished facilities, new administration, new staff, and a new feeling of family. Our winning streak instilled a sense of pride that was missing in the past, and it felt great to be a small part of it!

The new staff members were excited, too. For the first

time, students felt teachers cared about them. The power of positive thinking was clearly on display, and the staff approved a new school slogan—*We are Family!* The new slogan was only three small words, but they made all the difference. When I think about it, I can't think of another time more dynamic than my sophomore year. The school campus was refurbished, graffiti vanished, pipes hanging from the ceiling disappeared, central heat and air were installed, and the hallways were painted a cool gray. Complementing it was a winning varsity football team! The future of Blount High School appeared bright, and there was a good reason for optimism. However, if my school were going to have a complete reversal of fortune, it still had a big hurdle to overcome. The academic standing of Blount was still rated low, and standardized test scores were embarrassing—there was a big push from staff to improve. Such a dismal academic standing was Blount's biggest challenge, and we knew it would take time to rebound. After all, the school performed at a substandard level for years and, as I said before, change is never easy.

My personal life changed at that time, and I was no longer the scrawny little freshman of the previous year. I was a legitimate athlete, respected by my peers, and performing at a high level. I gained body weight and muscle mass from weightlifting over the summer, so I was bigger and stronger than the year before. I lead the team in receptions and receiving yards, and I was considered an impact player. With that designation came a considerable amount of responsibility and popularity and, as a direct result, my social life changed, too. When I wasn't consumed with athletics, I still had a keen interest in the girls. Marilyn Smith was my girlfriend at the start of the year, but our relationship was off and on, and we struggled to last through the year. Even when we broke up after having a disagreement we still remained friends, carrying on as if we were still a couple even when we knew we were no more than friends.

During one of our many breakups, I began to date Tonya Cauldwell, a cheerleader who was one grade level ahead of me. I met her through her cousin who ran freshman track with me, and both lived with her grandparents near Queen's Court. Some days after track practice I visited Rich, and stopped by her house to say hello. Now that I was playing varsity football, her cheerleading activities caused our paths to cross more often.

The news quickly spread around the school—Tonya and I were dating, and it really upset Marilyn. Even though we agreed to break up, Marilyn was obviously jealous knowing I was dating someone else. I made the situation worse when, for a brief time, I embraced Tonya as my girlfriend. Matters didn't get any better due to the fact that Marilyn played in the band, and Tonya was a cheerleader. They saw each other when practicing for the halftime shows and games, and I didn't help matters when I made a terrible mistake—I told each of them I would hang out with them after one of the games.

Not good.

Whenever I had a personal problem, I relied on Ty to help me out. He bailed me out several times before, and I decided to use him again. When I told him what I did, he decided to go out before me to check out the scene after the game. Upon his return, he reported both girls were waiting for me. He had an interesting way of expressing his point of view—he said, "Man, you better tie your shoes up tight, because we're going to have to run tonight!" My only question was, "Where am I going to run to?" There was only one way in and one way out of the campus, so I decided to hop the back gate to the school, and told Ty to pick me up in Grant's Circle.

Truth was I felt terrible—Tonya was my new girlfriend, and Marilyn was still one of my best friends. I didn't want to hurt their feelings, so I stood both of them up. At that moment, I didn't know what was more difficult—juggling the two girls, or dodging would-be tacklers!

In retrospect, I understand what my mom and dad went through in high school. I was becoming a reincarnation of my father—but, at that time, I didn't dwell on such things. I lived in the moment like most teenagers, and the only thing on my mind was the next big thing—the game with our crosstown rival, Vigor High.

Since we were having a great season, we hoped to use the momentum of our five-game winning streak to neutralize Vigor's undeniable advantage. They had a perfect 6-0 record in addition to the #1 national ranking. For us, a young program with a losing tradition, Vigor was our biggest challenge. It was exciting because it was the first time in many years people thought we had a chance to win.

I believe our early success was mainly due to Coach Harris. He was a good man, and well-respected in the community as a real family man. He and his wife were married for over ten years, and they had two young daughters. Coach Harris always encouraged us to do our best at whatever we were doing—at home, in the classroom, on the field, and in the weight room. As the season progressed, it was clear he was the closest thing many of us had to a role model and father figure. He spent much of his time trying to get to know us on a personal level, counseling us on issues off the field, and trying to give us fatherly advice surrounding our social affairs. Since the majority of his players were slated to graduate in the spring, he dedicated the Blount-Leflore game—traditionally played as the last game of the season for both schools—to them.

The Leflore football team wasn't very good, even though they suited up over sixty players for the game. We put up a good fight in the first half, but, once again, their numbers got the best of us in the second half. In the waning moments of the game there was an altercation, and both benches spilled onto the field. It ended up being an all-out fistfight with helmets flying, and water coolers being used as weapons. Our team was small, but we were feisty! We were ready for such a situation, and we got our share of punches in before officials, coaches, and stadium security broke up the fight. After the teams separated, we boarded the bus and headed back to our school campus— once we were in the locker room, Coach Harris was all over us! He was furious, yelling about our being low class, and poor sportsmen. He also put us on notice that such behavior wouldn't be tolerated, and anyone involved in a fight would be punished the following week during camp. Camp required us to do extra sprints, duck walks, crawls, and whatever else Coach could think of as punishment after already practicing for several hours. It was brutal, and camp definitely taught everyone involved a valuable lesson.

When the time came to match up with Vigor on the field, Coach Harris had us prepared. As usual, Prichard Stadium was filled with an overflow crowd that came to see that year's match up between crosstown rivals. We trotted onto the field, determined to make a statement—we did. Vigor may have expected another walkover, but we started out well, played them to a scoreless tie at halftime, and we left the field, dead even.

Yet again, however, there was strength in numbers, and the Vigor roster reflected it. They suited up eighty players to our thirty, and it was a war of attrition in the second half. Our stamina wore thin, and Vigor totally dominated us, walking away with a lopsided victory.

The final score was 33-0.

The game result was terrible, but I took pride in the fact I played my heart out. Not only did I catch a few passes, I also made an interception on defense. Besides, we lost to a team that went on to win the high school national championship that year.

After the loss, Coach Harris gave us a great speech, telling us good teams always bounce back from a significant loss, and this was our chance to prove it to ourselves and our fans. The next weekend, we didn't let him down as we rebounded with a victory. Eventually, we finished the season with a 6-4 record and a 5A regional championship, with the last game being one of high drama against our other crosstown rival, John L. Leflore.

It ended with a backyard brawl.

****

The regular season ended, and we entered the 5A playoffs. Our first opponent was Atmore High School, the same team that beat us in the first game of the season—but, this time would be different. We beat them handily, and the victory sent us to the second round. It was the first playoff win for Blount in many years, and it was proof our team definitely improved! The atmosphere of the entire school was upbeat, and we were learning how it felt to be winners!

However, our victory celebration was short-lived.

When we returned to school the following Monday, we learned from Coach Harris our next opponent would be Greenville High, the defending 5A state champs. We also learned because we were undefeated in 5A games, we were to host the game. The pressure was on, but it was very exciting to be in that position!

The stadium sold out. When game day arrived, it was the biggest field I ever played on, and my entire family was there to cheer me on. The game ended up being competitive and we provided our fans exciting moments, but we lost 22-14. The game ended our first winning season, and the future of Blount football was looking bright, although we would lose a lot of talent from our senior class the following year.

Shortly after the season ended, I received notification that I was voted First Team All County as a wide receiver by the sportswriters in the area. It was a great accomplishment for me as it was my first year playing the position. In addition, I kept up my schoolwork, and my grades were excellent, too. The best part was my mom, the number one supporter of my football career, was very proud of me. She was familiar with most of the boys because they also played football with me, and the guys really respected her. She never missed a game, always enjoying being around the team. Eventually, she became a member and officer of the Blount Football Booster Club, as well as our unofficial team mom.

****

Basketball season followed football, and I lost interest in playing for the school, satisfied to only play football and run track. Both were enough for me. That year, track was slightly different than my freshman year—we had a new coach named Theodore Bradley, and it was my first year to run indoor track. Coach Bradley worked several years with our community youth league, and he was knowledgeable about the sport. At that time, Blount's indoor track team was the best of the 1 A - 6 A high school teams in the state.

Indoor track was different from outdoor track because the surface was usually made of wood, and the oval was much smaller—we had to run two laps indoors to one lap of an outdoor track. A distance runner might cut his race short by a lap if not paying attention, and indoor sprints were sixty meters versus one hundred meters for outdoor sprints—field events were the same.

That year, I didn't become a legitimate sprinter. I was more quick than fast, so speed wasn't my greatest asset. Quickness is good for football, but for track I needed to be fast to compete. Nevertheless, I was a factor on my track team, and we won the Indoor State Championship for the first time. I placed third in the state meet in long jump, and I was the alternate for our relay team. If one of the top four couldn't compete, I stepped up to take his place— that happened a lot because the fastest guy at the school suffered from chronic injuries. I worked out with the sprinters each day of practice, helping increase my overall speed. Although the objective was to run faster sprints in track, I knew the additional speed would be an invaluable asset on the football field.

Outdoor track season started in the spring, and our team practiced at Prichard Stadium, sharing the track with Vigor. It was common to set up track meets between the athletes from the two schools during practice and, because my house was close to the stadium, it was common for a few of my teammates to stop by after practice. My house was on a busy street, so people spotted us and dropped in—before we realized it, my yard was full of people.

Including girls.

My sister worked at the Mobile Airport as a security guard, and when she returned home after work she usually found our yard full of people. She didn't like it, and immediately called Mom to tell her what was going on. Of course, when Mom got home after work, I explained my teammates and their friends stopped by after practice, and she told me it wasn't a problem for her—as long as no one went in and out of her house tracking dirt on the rugs. So, our house became a regular hangout from that day on— plus, she didn't have a problem with girls being there, too, as long as she were home. And, that was the operative phrase—*as long as she were home.* My sister, however, was always upset about something, and it angered her when girls came by. Whenever she got home and found us with the ladies, she called Marilyn telling her, "Get over here as soon as you can." It was really none of my sister's business, but Marilyn was her favorite of all my girlfriends, and both believed in 'the sisterhood.' It was interesting—of all the girls I dated, Marilyn was the only one my mother allowed to be in the house when she wasn't home. She was a sweet and gentle girl, and she won my mother over. In fact, when we were a couple, I always made sure I didn't disrespect her by being with other girls in her presence. But, sometimes, when my mom or sister were trying to protect her, it got on my nerves because I thought she could protect herself.

Despite the continuous drama between my mom, sister, Marilyn, and me, our track season was a big success. We added the state title for outdoor track to the indoor championship, and our success left little doubt that Blount was the premier high school track team in the State of Alabama.

****

As summer returned, team members met at the school, and we'd work hard on football drills and fundamentals. We lost our starting QB to graduation, so I was the only one in the group who had any quarterback experience—plus, I knew the offensive plays. Although the coaches were forbidden to be on the field with us during the summer break, they came out and watched from a distance. Big Jack and I could always be found in the Blount weight room where we could work out on our own. But, after our lifting, only the skilled position players would get together to continue unsupervised practice on the field. Other than that, we were relegated to playing pick-up games in the hood.

There were many times when a few boys in Big Jack's hood would play pickup football games, but I wasn't allowed to play. They didn't want the starting player for Blount to play because they felt it was unfair to both teams. It was bittersweet, really, for it was the end of my sandlot career. Sherman Williams, a neighborhood football legend had been put to rest, so I focused my energy on the looming football season. I was under a great deal of pressure—expectations of Blount were high, and we had to do better than the year before.

It wasn't going to be easy.

At Blount High School, a losing football team was no longer an option!

Chapter 7
Old Habits

I t was suddenly the summer of '89, and my junior year was three months away. When you're a teenager, the future seems so distant—yet, I was already halfway through high school with two years under my belt.

Everything was good!

Things changed for me that summer—as I mentioned, I was no longer a part of football in the hood, although I had plenty of it left at the high school level. Expectations of Blount's football program were high, and Coach encouraged the varsity players to work hard over the summer. So, we hung out together, focusing our goals on the coming season.

The senior varsity players weren't as gifted as those of the class of '89. It was difficult to replace the talent we lost, but there was a glimmer of hope—my junior class had proven talent, and the sophomore class also had a few players with high potential. We also expected the incoming freshman class to throw in raw talent we could rapidly develop. After two years, there were only a few players left from my freshman year—unfortunately, two very talented players from that team, Rich Robinson and Ben Martin, weren't eligible to participate due to academic probation. Their ineligibility was disappointing, but I still thought we could be competitive as we headed into a new season.

Unlike previous summers, the summer of '89 turned out to be busy for me. Prichard sponsored an ongoing community project called the Job Training Program Association, and Coach Harris hired on as a supervisor for the program at Faulkner Technical College. The college wasn't far from my house, adjacent to Vigor High School, and its goal was to prepare young men and women for the workplace upon graduating from Blount High School.

During my sophomore year, Coach Harris became more like a father figure, taking a strong liking to Big Jack and me. By that time, Jack and I were such close friends that Coach Harris used both of our names together. If there were an issue, he said, "Sherman Williams and Big Jack did this," and "Sherman Williams and Big Jack didn't do that." It was like we were joined at the hip!

Shortly after summer started, Coach Harris asked us if we wanted to participate in the job-training program. Twelve weeks. Minimum wage. I jumped at the chance, but Big Jack declined. It wasn't hard to understand why—he loved to sleep in, and the job required him to get up early to go to work. I have to admit, I wasn't a morning person myself, but I was a hustler and saw dollar signs. It was too good of an opportunity for me to turn down.

In Alabama, the legal working age is sixteen. I was only fifteen then, but the job-training program at Faulkner allowed kids under the age of sixteen to participate. Coach Harris explained the program was set up in such a way to provide protection for us from the state labor laws. I worked as part of the twenty man custodial maintenance group, cleaning the Faulkner campus each day, and I was happy to learn one of the crew was my cousin! A year or two older than I, we called him Byrd and, since he had a car, he offered to pick me up each morning on the way to work.

What I didn't know was Byrd had a hidden agenda.

Everyone knew Coach showed me a little favoritism, even though he tried to hide it by being strict with me during working hours. Byrd knew picking me up each morning provided cover for when he was occasionally late for work—Coach gave him a pass since he perceived Byrd was going out of his way to help me. It worked, but we were actually on time, most days.

Byrd had a valid driver's license, but I didn't. I learned to drive without one, but I was rapidly approaching my sixteenth birthday which was the legal driving age in Alabama. Since I needed someone with a valid driver's license to accompany me to the DMV to take the written test, Byrd agreed to help me. He even gave me a copy of the manual he used to get his license. I passed the test, and received my driving permit one month before my sixteenth birthday. Soon, we established a routine whereby Byrd would pick me up in the morning and take me to work. Then, after work, I rode to the school with Coach Harris to work out with the other players on my team. This worked out great for me until one day when Coach Harris learned I had my driving permit.

Coach had a few things he needed to drop off at the back of the school in the bed of his truck, so he ordered me to take his keys, go around back, and drop off the materials—which I promptly did. I drove to the back of the school, put the truck in reverse, and slowly backed into the location where he needed to make the drop. Suddenly, there was a loud bang, and I hit the brakes! I jumped out, and it was only then I noticed the tailgate was down, sporting a brand new dent. Suddenly, I had a sickening feeling in my stomach as I realized there was nothing I could do about it.

The damage was done.

Having an accident in a moving vehicle, no matter how small the damage, is one thing. But when it's your coach's signature truck and he obviously loves it, you're at a loss for words. In fact, it was the only one of its kind in the entire city of Prichard, and whenever or wherever we saw it parked or on the road, we knew it was Coach's truck.

I couldn't think of what to do.

I didn't say a word. I was afraid he'd be upset— really upset—and he just might snap. So, I carried on as if nothing happened. As we were running set plays and going over pass routes, Coach suddenly came around the building, screaming my name. I was right—he was upset. Fortunately for me, I had all of my own boys there in case he snapped and went off on me. He was way too big for me to take on by myself.

Eventually, he calmed down and we reached an agreement that required me to pay for the damage. My wages earned on the custodial group would pay my debt, but he never fixed the truck while I was a student athlete at Blount. He just drove the truck with a dented tailgate from that day forward. The tailgate incident occurred on the final day of my job program, but I had to hear about it from my friends for a long time. Eventually, the curiosity and interest in the accident subsided, and it was time to fully concentrate on football.

When football season of my junior year finally rolled around, I was fully committed and passionate about the sport. Most of the players had some idea of what position they would play, but I was essentially one hundred percent certain where I would end up. After all, I was an all-star wide receiver from last year's offense, and the starting cornerback on defense.

My good friend, Lamont Davis, returned as one of our running backs, with Jason Black and Big Jack anchoring our offensive line—the rest of the spots were filled with last year's backup. Our backup QB from the year before was Jackson Pruitt—he was 6'4", and a very good basketball player who played football with me at Clark. He was also a member of my old group, and lived in the same neighborhood as Big Jack. I didn't know him well, but he wasn't a stranger. Coach Harris wanted to make him that year's starting QB, but Pruitt's skill level wouldn't allow it. He was a lefty, and his passes were rarely on target. The problem Coach faced was a lack of an obvious alternative to rewarding him the starting position. The only option seem to be a freshman kid who was a good athlete, but not quite ready to compete on the varsity level. He reminded me of myself when I was a freshman.

After the first couple weeks of practice, Coach Harris knew he had to do something strengthen the QB position, and during one of our scrimmages he decided to give me a try. I ran the offense during summer workouts and knew all the plays, but I was receiver and running back. Although I passed the ball well, I didn't consider quarterbacking my strong suit. Much to my surprise, during the scrimmage some of my old freshman magic came back to me. For me, quarterbacking was like riding a bike—you never forget. I completed passes, and picked up chunks of yardage when forced to scramble out of the pocket.

The magician was back!

The next day Coach kept me at the QB position, and had me running plays with the first-team offense. My teammates were excited about my playing the position, but I certainly wasn't tall enough or gifted enough to think of myself as a natural QB. Yet, there is one quality I possess over all others that qualified me to run the offense—leadership.

Perhaps my leadership skills were the reasons Coach trusted me—by this time, I was starting quarterback on offense, and starting cornerback on defense. Like Lamont, one of our senior co-captains who played both ways, I was set to make a big contribution to the team. In fact, Lamont and I were so similar in stature, as well as our overall look, people thought we were brothers when they saw us together. As such, it was no surprise we were both members of The Smurfs. I looked up to him because he was expected to earn a scholarship to college through his efforts on and off the field.

Right before the season started, I celebrated my sixteenth birthday. Like so many teenagers before me, reaching the age of sixteen means a new freedom because it was the legal age for a driver's license in Alabama. I couldn't wait to get my license, and I actually got it on my birthday. Although I was driving illegally for some time, it definitely felt good to be able to drive legally.

By this time, my sister to came back to Prichard from California. Her husband transferred to Germany, and she was spending a few months with us before she would join him. When she returned, she brought back the 1978 Dodge van that was in our family for years—my dad bought it as an anniversary present for Mom when they were still married. The van was one of a kind, and had quite a family history because my brother drove it when he was in high school, followed by my two sisters. Now it was my turn!

That van may have been one of the most distinctive vehicles in the Mobile area—bright orange with a mural of a man surfing in sky-blue water on the side. Something common in California, it was a sight to see in Alabama! After my sister temporarily moved in with us, my mother gave me the van to drive back and forth to school. By this time, my other sister got married and moved to Georgia.

It was a summer of significant changes.

My living situation was different, and I moved into my brother's room. Sadly, he rarely came around, and didn't support me during my high school athletic career. The only real support I received during my high school career was from my mother as well as my sisters when they were visiting. My sister who moved back in left me alone most of the time, and didn't bother to tell my mother what I was up to each and every day. She was supportive of me, although she missed out on most of my football career—nevertheless, I hoped she might be able to stay with us long enough to see a game or two of my upcoming season.

During that summer, our team became close friends. We hung out together on and off the field, as well as after our workouts. We hung out at Mom's, but sometimes I went to The Bottom with Jack, or Queen's Court with Rich. It seemed wherever I was, Jack and Rich were there, too—and, one other kid.

Darius.

Darius played with me on our freshman team, but gave up football after that. He wasn't the best influence on me because whenever we got together, he drank and smoked weed. He was a good dancer, though! I discovered he and another guy from his neighborhood formed a dance group called The Heavy Heads, a group named after their signature dance moves. It wasn't long before I started hanging around with them so much that they asked me to become a member of their group. After that, we entered talent shows throughout the city, and often won cash prizes, winning more often than not! Eventually, I couldn't stay with the dance group since football was my number one priority. Our final performance was in the school talent show, and most of my fellow students were surprised to see me perform as a dancer. We lost the competition, and that was the end for me.

It was time to focus on football.

Every football season is a mystery—my teammates were sidelined by injuries, athletic probation due to substandard academic performance, or just plain loss of interest in the sport. As we prepared for the first game of our season, Jason Black, our star running back, suffered a season-ending knee injury. Rich was also hurt during our training, although his loss didn't have the same impact as losing Black—he was a backup, and a special teams player.

Rich stayed away from practice for a few days, and eventually stopped altogether. I dropped by his house after practice to check on him, attempting to determine when he planned to return. It was a crapshoot whether he'd be there—if he weren't at his Mom's, I looked in his old Queen's Court neighborhood. Sure enough, I found him there on the block hanging out with his homeboys, hustling, selling dope, smoking weed, and drinking. As usual. Although they offered me something, I declined during football season because I didn't want to make such vices a regular habit. I wasn't against celebrating a game victory—but, after the game was over, their behavior became a daily ritual.

I found Rich, and asked how things were going. He responded his knee was still hurting, but he would be back as soon as it healed. Well, his injury must never have healed, because he definitely never came back! Every once in a while, he returned to school, but eventually he dropped out completely. I knew he was making a big mistake, but we remained good friends after he left school. Since I had my own wheels, I knew whenever I felt like it I could drive to Queen's Court to hang out, have a drink, and smoke some weed.

Although we lost Rich, the rest of my team stayed reasonably intact. Sometime right before school started, we formed a clique known as 'Da Fellas,' made up of only the guys from my class of '91. I don't think my mother ever expected the van she gave me for transportation to go to and from school would serve as a limo service for Da Fellas. But, it was perfect for the job! We piled up in the van and cruised around the city and, after our games, we hit the local spots where the black kids headed for their post-game parties.

My van was so unique and well known at McDonald's on Wilson Avenue and Godfather's Pizza on Dauphin Street, none of my peers could miss it. And, everywhere I went, if there were likelihood of trouble, I carried my problem solver. I guess it provided me a sense of protection for myself and all of my friends in the van. This was especially true when Marilyn and her girlfriends would tag along after our games. It seemed harmless—Marilyn and the girls tagging along—but Marilyn always dressed in her cheerleading outfit, having become a member of the squad that year. I knew wearing the cheerleader outfit could cause unintended consequences because it had the possibility of attracting negative attention by students or gang members from rival schools. It was my responsibility to keep her safe.

Tonya was a cheerleader, too, but she seldom joined in

with us. She and I parted ways earlier that year—she was a senior slated to graduate, and staying together never would have worked out. Nevertheless, before, during, and after the games, I think Marilyn wanted to ride with me to keep an eye on the situation. I can't say I blame her, and it didn't bother me in the least.

The anticipation of our football team making a run for the State Championship was high—the town and students wanted us to build on the success we had in the playoffs. The buzz was 'The Magician' was maturing and would be starting at the QB position. Having just celebrated my sixteenth birthday, my driver's license, inheriting the family van, and forming Da Fellas, it was impossible not to be excited and a little egotistical all at the same time! Our success was contagious, and it inspired the parents of Blount High to form a Boosters Club for the football team. It meant for the first time parents would travel to away games as a group. The theme of 'we are family' was taking hold, and even some of the local drug dealers who were former students of Blount high began to support our program.

The local dealer sponsored and organized caravans and trips for people who wanted to travel to the away games, but couldn't afford it. Perhaps their generosity was pay back to the community that suffered from their drug trade—they filled their pockets with money that should have been spent on Prichard family needs instead of their drugs. These trips, however, were more like a party for the dealers. Most drug dealers in the Prichard area were huge sports fans, and many of them played sports, but they were sidelined by injury, or couldn't meet the demands of the classroom. I knew some of them, and they knew me— some played sandlot football with me when I was younger.

Junior year? Good memories. Prichard recognized me

as an elite football player, and I was popular in my hood. Anyone high school, or a fan of football knew me.

In retrospect, maybe it wasn't such a good thing for a boy of sixteen.

****

Robert John, a major drug dealer in Prichard, was a big fan of Blount football, sponsoring most of the away game trips. It was my success in football and his success in drugs that forged our friendship—a friendship suspect from the beginning. He constantly pressured me for information about our upcoming games, the game plan, what we saw on film, and what we expected from the other team. To this day, I'm not sure what he did with the information, but it seemed as if he were a bookie, hedging bets. The only positive outcome was that I was motivated to study game films much closer than ever before—I wanted to answer his questions, and, in the long run, it made me a much better student of the game.

First Avenue was the area of Prichard where drug dealers lived, hung out, and sold. Most of the kids living on First Avenue were Blount students and, before long, I met Jeremy James. He was a Blount student who lived on First Avenue and worked with Robert John. We became friends, and Jeremy became a go-between for Robert John and me. He routinely passed messages while we were at school, the majority of them a simple request to stop by John's house to give them information on this week's game plan.

My reward? A crisp $100 bill we called 'gas money.'

Every time I went to meet with Robert John, Jeremy

would be somewhere nearby, although he wouldn't attend our meetings. I realized later that everyone knew exactly when I visited John, and how often. My van was so uniquely identifiable, I couldn't park anywhere near the house without everybody in town noticing. I never thought to hide it, and I'm pretty sure hiding it was impossible, anyway. Soon, word got out to Coach Harris that I was visiting Rich and his homeboys in Queen's Court, and Robert John on first Avenue. The implication was clear—I was selling drugs.

The next thing I know, Coach Harris called me into his office to tell me people spotted my van parked in areas of high drug activity for long periods of time. The air was thick with tension, and I assured him I wasn't dealing drugs, or having any part of it.

We left it at that.

****

Robert John was a very charismatic person, and his ultimate goal was for us to win the State Championship so he would have bragging rights over the other drug dealers in the city. And, his ultimate strategy to accomplish a championship was to find ways to motivate me to perform at a very high level. It worked. By the end of the season, I passed for over 1500 yards, rushed for over 1000 yards, scored 20 touchdowns, and had several interceptions on defense. Adding it up, I earned over $3000 from Robert John's incentives, and that didn't include the gas money.

In spite of my accomplishments, we weren't winning— not even coming close to meeting everyone's expectations.

Disappointed, we didn't make the playoffs. It seemed as if we reverted back to the losing ways of the old Blount High, and we finished the season with four wins and six losses. Or, it may have been the simple fact that we partied too often during the season to realistically expect a winning outcome.

After the season ended, all we could do was focus on next year. Fortunately, only four senior players graduated, and wouldn't be back. One of them was Lamont, and I was sorry to see him go—but the loss of players from the senior class was offset by my returning, varsity teammates, and new additions. We brought talented players from the sophomore class, and we added a good crop of players from our freshman team. We even looked forward to several players transferring from other schools. Everyone would make a contribution and, if there were no surprises, I felt we would have a solid and experienced team for my senior year.

After football ended, the team continued to hang out together. When we traveled as a group, I drove the van, and sometimes Lamont and I went off by ourselves to pick up girls. Since my van was well known and easy to spot, I enjoyed cruising around in his car instead of mine. Much more low-key. The bad thing was Lamont was dating a member of the cheerleading squad, a teammate of Marilyn's, and it was a bit difficult to sneak around without her hearing about it (girl chasing was one of my main weaknesses.) What seemed an innocent activity to me eventually ended up with unintended consequences that would last for years.

We found out our girl chasing caused a big conflict with the guys in other neighborhoods. Since neighborhoods in Prichard are territorial, seeing or dating girls outside of our own immediate community was considered off-limits. When Lamont and I crossed neighborhood boundaries to chase girls, it literally set up a war between the boys in our neighborhoods.

It all started one day when Big Jack, Clarence DeMott, and a few of Da Fellas and I were driving my van through the city, and we spotted a few girls walking down the street—so we decided to double back, and cut them off of at the next street over. I was driving, Big Jack rode shotgun, and Clarence was in the back of the van with some of the other guys. By now, Jack's nickname was 'Big Friendly' and, although most of the time he was a gentle giant, at times he didn't live up to the meaning of his new name.

A group of boys who lived in the area we were cruising called themselves The BBV—an abbreviation for the Boys Behind Vigor, our foremost inner-city school rival. Since most of the kids attending Vigor also went to Clark, we knew them well. When we finally caught up to the girls, they kept walking and we continued to drive slowly, keeping pace. As we moved along, a few of the BBV came out of their homes to meet the girls, and take care of any impending situations. We soon found out the girls we were pursuing were girlfriends of several of the guys in the BBV.

They asked if there were a problem, and one girl said no. Then, for whatever reason, Clarence decided to defend the Da Fellas' honor—why, I'm not sure, but it may have been he was offended by the question posed to the girls by the BBV. He grabbed my problem solver and jumped out of the van, pointing and waving it in the air. As if that weren't bad enough, he confronted them by asking if they had a problem.

The BBV retreated, but the confrontation had just begun.

It was war.

There was no question that all of us were in danger. We lived in the greater Prichard area, so there was really no way to avoid each other, and it was the minor confrontation that turned our town into the wild West. Whenever we crossed paths, it was shoot to kill, and, ironically, one of the girls we tried to pick up that day was Marla Brown.

She later became the mother of one of my children.

From that day forward, things were dangerous. The only thing separating the geographic area of the two school districts was a railroad track. Everyone on both sides of the tracks understood if we crossed them, we were entering a danger zone. So, the two groups avoided each other as much as possible and, luckily, we seldom crossed paths at high school games or house parties around the city.

Then it got crazy. The BBV shot Lamont.

It happened during Mardi Gras season when the local fair was in town. Lamont and a few of Da Fellas were hanging out at the fair when they were spotted by the BBV. Without warning, the BBV opened fire, and Lamont took a bullet in his kidney. Word was the bullets were meant for me, and the BBV shot Lamont by mistake—the obvious downside to looking alike.

When I received a phone call about the shooting, I immediately rushed down to the fairgrounds armed with my problem solver. It was over by the time I arrived, and Lamont was on his way to the hospital. The good news was he underwent surgery to remove his kidney, and he survived. The bad news was in two weeks he was scheduled to sign for his athletic scholarship to attend the University of Southern Mississippi.

Later that night, Da Fellas, and Lamont's neighborhood friends met up to come together as one with one purpose in mind—revenge. Retaliation was a must and, in the wee hours, we called in all available weapons.

The following day, the BBV shot a young boy who lived in Clarence's neighborhood in retaliation for our work the night before. And, so began a cycle of violence. A few weeks later, they caught Big Friendly near the railroad tracks, and shot him in the butt. When he was examined at the hospital, the doctor said his butt was so big that the bullet lodged deep into the tissue, and it would cause too much damage to remove it. Ever.

The railroad tracks served as a boundary to keep Da Fellas and the BBV apart, but Da Fellas would still get together for house parties. Although we would hear of house parties being held on Vigor's side of the tracks, we didn't attend. Likewise, when the BBV heard about our parties, they didn't cross the tracks.

I hosted many of the parties, and we hired a DJ, printed fliers, and passed them out to invite kids from all over the city of Mobile—although, due to its violent reputation, most people weren't keen to visit Prichard. My parties brought kids from all around, and I used my mother's garage as a dance area, and the yard served as a lounge where everybody could hang out. Security was provided by some of my guys with guns, posting themselves up the street surrounding the house in case any troublemakers showed up.

We charged a cover, and served free beer from a keg. Some of the kids would bring their own bottles of beer or liquor and, for those who didn't want beer, we had a spiked punch. We hid the keg of beer in a corner of the yard where it was dark and secluded, so if my mother or sister came out to check on things, we covered up or hid the kegs.

These parties were lots of fun and, fortunately, no one ever got hurt at any of them. But, the downside was everyone knew where I lived, and Mom's house was a potential target of the BBV. At times, I sat on top of the house with a .22 caliber rifle after hearing a rumor of a planned drive-by shooting. I had to protect my mom, sisters, nieces, and nephew, as well as Mom's property. I guess I overreacted because they never did drive by—yet, in the midst of all the ongoing shootings, I felt I couldn't be too careful.

****

In the midst of all these goings-on, Marilyn got pregnant. I was in shock when she told me, and I shrugged it off. I knew she wasn't feeling well, but I thought she was sick—only not with morning sickness! Of course, I heard all the stories about teen pregnancy in high school, and I always used condoms, but I never thought it would happen to me. So, when it finally sunk in, I contemplated what we should do. I was only sixteen years old, and I knew nothing about being a father! And, the way things were going in Prichard, I wasn't sure I would live to see my next birthday. So many questions—*how will I break the news to my mother? Her parents? How will her father, who is very strict, take the news? He didn't like me before he knew about the pregnancy—what will he think?* My mind was flying!

I remember thinking I only had to deal with my mother. Poor Marilyn lived with her father and mother, and she would have to deal with both of them. Nonetheless, I put all that aside, and focused on the solution for us to solve the problem—I believed her only option was an abortion.

I wasn't ready to become a father, but I wasn't sure how Marilyn felt about it. I realized it wasn't just my problem, it was our problem, and we had to talk about the options.

Together.

The first thing we did was call several different abortion clinics, but none would perform an abortion on a minor without parental consent. It seemed we were backed into a corner, and we decided we had no other option but to run the idea by my sister. Just the thought of telling her upset my stomach—she could never keep a secret, and I knew it was a mistake to tell her. We considered going directly to Mom, but it made sense for my sister to run interference.

By this time, Marilyn was desperate, and she convinced me we should ask my sister's advice. I reluctantly agreed, and it went down as I expected—within one hour, my mother said she wanted to talk to us, and it was no surprise when she demanded to know what was going on. An hour after that, all of us were sitting down in front of Marilyn's parents. I was frightened, but very relieved my mother was there because I was relatively sure she wouldn't let Marilyn's father kill me.

Marilyn's parents were fairly calm after having been hit with the bombshell. Her mother was asking Marilyn the obvious—why? Then the conversation turned to me asking how I planned to take care of the baby. I told them the same thing I told my mom—I would get a job.

And, that's exactly what I did.

First, I contacted my cousin Byrd. He worked at a seafood restaurant, and he told me they were looking for some good help. We met up at the restaurant, and I filled out the application. The next day, I was bussing tables on the night shift. It was okay—I worked there for a few months, and met some good people. In particular, Carl Washington. Carl attended Blount a few years before me, and I thought he was cool. He was a popular drum major for the Blount marching band, and quite the ladies' man. He introduced me to quite a few very nice girls and, on occasion, all of us spent time together drinking beer and smoking weed. One night, while Carl and I were looking for weed, I suggested we drive over to see my friend Rich. Since his days on the football team, he became a full-fledged drug dealer, so I figured he could supply our needs. Both of us wore our work uniforms, and looked out of place when we showed up in Queen's Court. When we pulled up, I noticed everyone looked suspicious when they didn't recognize Carl's car. When I got out, I asked why they were acting funny, and they told me the only thing they saw when we drove off was a guy in uniform. They mistook us for The Folks—a slang term used to describe the undercover police who worked in the neighborhood in unmarked cars.

After they realized who we were, they settled down. If we turned out to be officers in the drug task force, they would've taken off running. It wasn't unusual to see the chase going on in the hood and, if any of them were caught holding drugs, they were taken in and interrogated for information. In fact, that was how most of the drug conspiracy cases were put together starting with the users, then to the street dealers, and finally to the big-time suppliers. Most of the time, it ended in a grand jury indictment.

One of the boys volunteered to get Rich for me, and before long he showed up. He was surprised to see me in my restaurant uniform, and I explained to him that I now had a job.

"A job? Why do you need a job?"

I explained Marilyn was pregnant. Friend that he was, he didn't hesitate to offer me a job immediately as he flashed a bankroll of money. It was tempting, but I still had strong ethics. Besides, my focus was on building my football career, and taking care of my responsibilities to Marilyn and our unborn child. It wouldn't do either of us any good if I ended up juvenile criminal detention. So, I told him I appreciated his offer, and explained my need for some weed. Rich was clearly disappointed with my answer, but he sent one of these homeboys to get whatever I needed. We left with a few days' supply, and a personal promise from Rich that if I ever changed my mind about working for him, I knew where to find him. It seemed to me Rich was never going back to school, but I told him he was still one of Da Fellas, and a member of our football team.

"You need to be ready to play when the season starts," I told him. Yet, in my heart, I knew he really wasn't interested in playing football anymore.

After working at the restaurant for a short time, I realized I wasn't cut out for bussing tables. It was a real drag. Going to school all day long, working out for football in the afternoon, and heading off to work at night wasn't what I wanted for my life. It was inevitable Rich's offer would put more money in my pocket than I could earn bussing tables, and thinking about it overwhelmed my thoughts. One night after work, I drove to Queen's Court to see Rich, parked my van a few blocks away, and walked the remaining distance—I didn't want my van to be seen anywhere near Rich's territory. When I found him, we talked, smoked, and drank beer. Before long, his regular customers who were mostly addicts approached us to make a purchase.

The way drugs changed hands on the street was rather simple. Rich pulled out a bag of crack cocaine in the form of white pebbles, dug in, and handed the dope to the drug fiends. In return, he they gave him cash. It seemed simple. Straightforward. In no time bussing was out, and we spent the rest of the time discussing the details of how we would work together.

When I got paid that Friday, I drove to the local convenience store to cash my check, then I headed back to Queen's Court and kicked it with Rich. I told him I was going to buy in to see how selling drugs could work for me.

He understood my position—not enough money, or more money than I could imagine. So, I used my weekly earnings to purchase a supply of crack for resale. When I think about it, I'm amazed by how quickly I compromised my ethics and values to make easy money. I never planned to get sucked into the dark world of street dealing, but a series of bad choices punctuated by Marilyn's pregnancy caught up with me and clouded my thinking. By this time, Marilyn worked at McDonald's so after school I took her to work—then home, parked my van, and jumped on my bike to ride over to Queen's Court. I didn't want the van around when I was hustling with Rich and his homeboys.

The money was flowing in, and Rich and I decided to host a party at his mother's house during school hours. We invited a bunch of girls, and partied with Da Fellas as well as allowed a few other boys from our class who just transferred to Blount to attend. One of them was Mike Tobias, and another was Mitchell Mobley—they were cool, and we all started to hang around together. When it came time for our party, a few of the guys in Rich's mom's neighborhood heard about it. They attended Blount, but weren't part of the athletic scene or Da Fellas.

They crashed.

By the time they showed up, Mike was pretty drunk, and he slammed the door on them when they tried to push their way in. He told him they weren't welcome and, when they left, they were upset. Not a good sign, and I should've known the incident wasn't over. The next morning when I arrived at school the stage was set—a big fight ensued between us and the guys who tried to crash our party.

It was common for fights to break out at school on occasion, but this was more like a war. Prior to the party, the tension was building between us for months—but, when Mike slammed the door in their faces, it was the straw that broke the camel's back. The fighting spread throughout the school, fortunately confined to fistfights rather than dodging bullets. The one exception was a thrown chair that hit a guy I knew, splitting his head open, requiring stitches.

The situation lasted several hours, and it was out of control until the police arrived. Every time the police stopped me, I broke free and ran to a different part of the school to continue to fight. By the end of the day, I was 'cuffed and stuffed,' and carted away to the juvenile detention center. The next day, all the students who actively participated in the fight were expelled from school for the rest of the year. Including me.

Mom was furious! After arranging my release from juvie, she took my keys to the van. She was right—I deserved it. But what she didn't realize was that I still had my bike, and I could ride it to Queen's Court each day while she was at work.

Since having the van at my disposal didn't make a difference, I continued to hustle with Rich on most days since I was no longer attending school. No more classes, homework, or afternoon football practices. No more weekend games at Prichard Stadium in the near future. All I had left was my Queen's Court hustle.

It's an often told story in the black communities of Alabama—a young African-American boy of sixteen who got into trouble with the law, expelled from school, and was hustling each day.

It was all I had to do.

Chapter 8
State Championship

The summer of 1990 was bizarre. After the events of my junior year ended with my expulsion for the remainder of the academic year, I experienced uncertainty going into my last year at Blount. Would I be eligible to play football?

Fortunately, Coach Harris was well-respected by the school administration, and his word carried a lot of weight. He went to bat for me during my eligibility hearing, convincing the administration to allow the grades I earned up to the point of my expulsion to be entered as part of my official school records. He argued the administration denied me the chance to take my final exams to pull up any of my non-passing grades. I carried a solid 3.0 grade point average since the second quarter of my freshman year, and he expected no less for me had I completed my classes. Yep—Coach Harris was darned convincing! Ultimately, the administration reinstated my eligibility— but, my teammates weren't so lucky. Big Friendly was a key player on our football team as well as one of my closest friends, but that didn't make a difference. Our friendship didn't score points with the school administration, forcing him to attend night school as a condition of his eligibility reinstatement. Since Big Friendly and I were inseparable, I did whatever I could to help him, and he would do the same for me. Everything that went on at Blount was associated with the two of us one way or another—we were members of Da Fellas, played football, and hung out in the hood together.

Attending night classes required Big Friendly to commute across town to Murphy High School and, since he didn't have transportation, I took him and picked him up. It was a good thing I had the van because Big Friendly was too big to comfortably fit in any of our friends' cars. I didn't mind, though—my Big Friendly limo service turned out to work well for me because as I waited for him to finish class, I took the opportunity to visit a girl who ran track for Murphy. It was a pleasant way to pass the time, and I enjoyed her company because both of us were interested in sports.

Big Friendly eventually passed night classes with high enough grades to earn his eligibility. By this time, he was a habitual smoker and, as a consequence, I started to smoke more. It wasn't good for our health or stamina on the football field, but it was part of the culture of cruising around town. During that summer, Da Fellas seized every opportunity to have a good time, and we plugged into all the local activities. Whenever we heard of someone having a party, we crashed it to meet girls, drink beer, smoke weed, and hang out. We still frequented the skating rink, but in 1990 the Festival Center was our favorite place to get together. It was a two screen movie theater charging only a buck for admission, and it attracted a diverse group of teenagers from around the greater Mobile area—a perfect spot to settle gang rivalries, and many nights ended with fistfights or shootouts.

One night, a friend and I were hanging out at the dollar movie when we spotted a very attractive girl standing with her friends, so I told my friend I was going to approach her to try to hook up with her.

The girls' names were Sharkita and Jasmine, and Sharkita was a couple years younger than I. In casual conversation, I learned she lived in Batesfield which was a good distance from Prichard, and she attended Laker High School. I think we figured we wouldn't see each other much, but we swapped phone numbers and started a long-distance friendship. At first we talked on the phone, but, as time went on, I made the long drive to her parent's house. Sometimes, we split the distance by meeting at the Festival Center.

Sharkita's parents were Jamaican, and both spoke English with a heavy accent. Her mother liked me, and invited me over for dinner on occasion—she was a good cook, and treated me extremely well. Visiting Sharkita's house provided me an opportunity to escape from the cruel reality of Prichard—I felt different when I visited Sharkita's, and maybe one reason was because they weren't US citizens. Or, maybe it was they had no previous knowledge of my struggles on the streets in and around Prichard. Whatever the reason, I didn't worry about my past behavioral issues or excess baggage when I was a guest in their house. They were under the impression I was a good kid. A decent kid.

I think Sharkita's family was an excellent influence on me. Visiting Batesfield allowed me to see another side of life away from Prichard, and it felt good to be welcomed in their home. I always strove to maintain a clean image with Sharkita's parents as a way to build up trust between us. With trust comes responsibility, and Sharkita's parents trusted me to pick her up, and take her on dates without a chaperone. I had to step up and take on the responsibility from a safety perspective. Since she lived so far away from Prichard, my orange van didn't function as a magnet attracting trouble. In fact, sometimes I drove to Batesfield and left my problem solver at home. But, I always had to drive back to Prichard to face the reality of my day-to-day life. When I think about it, my time with Sharkita was some of the best of my high school years.

****

Most of the guys in Prichard had some type of weapon. When Big Friendly and I rode together, he liked to have my problem solver sitting in his lap—there was little doubt after being shot in the butt he was a little paranoid. He was always ready to bust at the first sign of drama, and the ongoing war with the BBV made it imperative to always be on guard.

It was never good to get caught sleeping in the hood.

Those weren't the only events that made the summer of 1990 bizarre—my mother remarried, and both of my sisters were in the transition phase. They were back living at Mom's with their kids while their husbands were overseas on active military deployment. The house went from being just my mother and me to being fully occupied. As a teenage guy, it was a tough adjustment for me, so I developed a habit of finding things do to in order to keep away from the everyday chaos of family life. I even looked for ways to spend as much time away from the city of Prichard as possible.

Mom and her new husband seemed to get along well, and I didn't have an issue with the marriage—he was an ex-cop who decided to become a truck driver. We talked a lot, and I thought he was pretty cool for an ex-cop. Such kitchen-table conversation was in stark contrast to the life I led away from my family—in that life, cops were the enemy. It was during that time I started to develop a dislike for driving the orange van. It seemed everyone knew my van so well that I couldn't drive anywhere without attracting attention. So, I started to develop the habit of riding my bike to visit people nearby or crosstown, and Marilyn's house was only a ten-minute walk from Mom's property. Even when I needed to drive Marilyn to work, I borrowed one of my sister's vehicles, then I hustled using the borrowed car after I dropped Marilyn off at work. I was taking my responsibilities seriously, but I still continued my illicit behavior—life was still about Marilyn, my unborn child, and dealing drugs.

That summer, the family became aware my older brother was a drug addict. I figured it out for myself earlier, though I didn't know at the time he was using crack. Had I known, I might've told my mom, but the thought of snitching on my own brother didn't set well with me. He knew I was hustling, and tried to cover up his habit for me by pretending he was also hustling. And, he hustled for me for a while. But, eventually I figured it out despite the fact we never established a big brother relationship. I think our age gap played a big part in preventing us from being close. He didn't live in Prichard, but he came home through Queen's Court to get his drugs once in a while. When there was a drought or interruption in the supply, he used his personal connections to get what he needed. His drug addiction was obvious, and all of us witnessed his life spinning out of control when he drove to my mother's house, stole her TV and VCR, stole my sisters' video cameras, and several other items.

Mom was disappointed to discover her oldest child was a drug addict so desperate for money he could steal from his own family. There was no other choice but to confront him, so everyone piled into my mom's car and drove out to his apartment. When they arrived, his girlfriend greeted us, and confirmed she saw my brother with the stolen merchandise. She broke down while explaining state of their drug addiction to my mom and sisters. Although my mother was upset, she still wanted to help both of them—but, at that point, there wasn't a thing she could do.

It was too late.

Eventually, my brother promised to pay them back for what he took, but he never did. I had the unfortunate experience of witnessing all the pain of the situation and how it broke my mother's heart. The whole thing had an interesting effect on me, though—I reflected on what I was doing, and stopped hustling for a few days. My intentions were admirable, but intentions don't mean squat in real life. The reality was I needed money to pay all the associated expenses related to Marilyn's pregnancy. And, in the hood, hustling was the quickest and easiest way to make money.

I was making my fair share.

Looking back, it was a valuable childhood lesson. I always looked up to my brother as a Superman figure, and although I dealt with many different types of dope fiends during my childhood, I always believed drug addiction could only happen to weak-minded people. But, when it broke Superman down, I realized it could happen to anybody—from that day forward, I viewed crack cocaine as kryptonite. I guess every crisis has its upside because after things settled down, I vowed to myself I wouldn't experiment with drugs other than marijuana. I already crossed the line with recreational use, and there was no undoing that. As I flashed back to my days when my brother was still living at home, I wished I could've helped him to make the same decision for himself.

After all the turmoil, my brother stayed away from the family for a while. My sisters soon moved out to join their husbands at their respective army bases and, again, an unexpected vehicle found its way to me. One of my sisters and her husband owned two Fort escorts—she drove her husband's car to their new home, and left her car behind to become part of my mother's yard. Since I wanted to get rid of the orange van . . .

I saved my money with plans to buy a brand-new car that summer. I made good money from hustling, and before long, I saved up $20,000. I figured that was enough money to buy a used Mercedes-Benz or BMW, so a couple of Da Fellas and I went car shopping. We were pretty successful, and located a few late models in good condition. At the time, they were the types of cars successful hustlers drove, as well as vehicles that focused heat on their drivers in the hood. Not many people in Prichard made enough money to purchase these types of cars, and it was a foregone conclusion that the owners were engaged in some type of career criminal activity. Everyone, including the local police, identified them with drug dealers, and that's when it dawned on me I was in the game for the money.

I believed my hustling would be short-lived because I was hustling only as a temporary solution to my immediate my needs. So, purchasing one of these expensive models wouldn't only deplete my entire savings, it would put me right back where I was before. What good is a fancy car with no cash on hand to pay for my current and future obligations?

The myth surrounding the hustle stated that once individuals got in, they could never get out. I didn't want that, so I was bound and determined to shatter the myth. I wasn't into letting someone give me anything—what I wanted or needed, I bought. I wasn't going to be in someone's debt. When I first went to Rich, I bought in with my own cash money. And, when the time came for me to walk away, I wanted it to be on my terms with no obligations to anybody.

One of the main reasons I wanted to buy a new car was the van got into . . . situations. It became obvious to me one day when Marilyn and I were driving to the mall to shop for senior class rings—it was late in her pregnancy, and hiding her big belly was impossible. Whenever I had her with me, I made every effort to avoid all dangerous areas of the city. I also made sure there were no drugs in the van, and I left my problem solver with Big Friendly. On this particular day, when we were driving home from the mall, my decision to keep myself unarmed and my van clean paid dividends. I needed gas, so I pulled off into one of the Prichard gas stations known for high drug traffic. When I pulled in, a drug task force consisting of ten to fifteen cars with officers rolled up on us. They swarmed everywhere, pointing guns, and shouting, "Hands in the air! Get out of the vehicle, and get on the ground!"

Marilyn was terrified. When I looked over at her, she was crying. That really upset me, and I started yelling back, "My girlfriend is pregnant! You better not do nothing to hurt her, or my child!" By this time, I was on the ground being cuffed—there was little I could do. They started pushing me around asking questions such as, "Where are the guns and drugs?" I shouted back I didn't have any idea what they were talking about, and I didn't have anything. A different officer started searching the van and, in the end, they found absolutely nothing and had to let us go.

I dodged a bullet.

After the showdown, I explained to Marilyn that someone must've put the police on me, and they were targeting my van. She didn't realize if she hadn't been with me, there was no telling what they might have found. But, instead of viewing the incident as a sign from God telling me to straighten myself out and stop hustling, I viewed it as a signal advising me to buy a new car.

A few weeks later, my sister called from Georgia to tell Mom she wanted to sell her Ford Escort. It was a compact car, low-key, and inexpensive. The timing was perfect, and it was just what I wanted—so, I bought it and saved the bulk of my cash.

After I purchased the Escort, I parked the van. I didn't want to get rid of it, because it was still useful to drive Big Friendly and Da Fellas even though some of them had their own vehicles. Most had their own problem solvers as well, and it seemed as if things were starting to settle down and fall into place.

The bizarre events of the summer of '90 were a turning point in my young life. Despite the hustling, fighting, dating, and hanging out, one thing that never changed was my passion for the game of football. Achievement of my personal goals for my senior year depended heavily on a rigorous personal training program, starting with track in the spring and, despite my daily activities, I committed myself to my best training. My time as a sprinter on the varsity track team the previous year paid off and, as a result, my foot speed improved tremendously. I became a mainstay on the 4 x 100 meter, also competing in the open sprint events, such as the 100 meter and mile relay team—100 meter and 200 meter, too. But even though I had my hands full with the sprint activities, I stayed true to my field events. My personal best came in the long jump, consistently placing in the top three spots. Coach and my teammates knew they could always count on me picking up points for the team at our local meets, as well as at the State Championship.

I developed a habit of training under the watchful eye of my coaches, as well as on my own. One way I built up my speed was to chase cars as they passed down my street. Most of them were driven by someone I knew, and since we lived on a one-way street, I lined up in the street waiting for a car to come by. When it approached and was about to pass, I took off running, trying to keep up. It was simple exercise that helped me to improve my speed, keeping me at top sprinting speed.

By the time spring flipped into summer, I immersed myself in an intense personal training program, and I put in as many hours of training as possible during daylight hours. I even put aside my car and bicycle, and ran to and from school as part of my daily workout routine—a great way to build my endurance.

When football season started again, I knew I would be playing both ways, but I wasn't sure of the position—Coach played me at quarterback during my junior year, but he also played me at strong safety position at times. Apparently, he didn't want his quarterback to play cornerback where injury was more likely than at safety. This caused a dilemma because I was the best cover man he had, and also one of the best tacklers on the defense team. The fact was he needed me on offense and defense.

I figured everything was set to play quarterback and strong safety until one day Coach Harris and Coach Parker called me to their office for a talk. They told me they were changing me to running back on offense, and it was my job to find my replacement at quarterback. I also had to teach the position during the summer. For some reason, Coach Harris decided to go back to the offense we used during his first year at Blount. Since I was a running quarterback and racked up over 1000 yards rushing the year before, it seemed the transition to running back wouldn't be too difficult.

My first thought for my replacement at QB was Farley Love, but he took ill and wasn't able to play that year. So I started to contact the boys on the freshman team from the year before—I really didn't have a lot of options in mind. After Farley, there was a freshman kid who caught my eye—in my view, he showed some athleticism on the field when he played defensive line. During the summer workouts, he told me he wanted to try out for varsity at one of the skilled positions. He and a friend from his neighborhood showed up every day at summer workouts, and I recognized their dedication. I respected it.

I decided to line them up with six to eight other boys whom I thought showed promise. I had each of them throw the ball to determine who might be a viable QB candidate, but none of them could throw the ball over thirty yards. We worked together on passing techniques for days and weeks without any progress, but the kid I had my eye on separated himself from the rest simply by learning all the offensive plays.

By the time the team reached the two-practices-a-day schedule for varsity, the kid realized his job would be simple. With me at running back and the new run-based offense of Coach Harris, all he had to do was learn the plays and hand me the ball. So, despite his lack of passing skill,

I took him under my wing and taught them how to be a quarterback. Eventually, his dedication overcame his lack of skill, and he went on to be a better QB than I ever was.

Eventually, varsity summer camp started, and Coach started me at the QB position with the first-team offense. The kid was assigned to run the second-team offense until Coach was comfortable enough to let him take over the first team. During the transition period, we used a running back by committee—the starting running back returned from a season ending knee injury the previous year, but he maintained his size and strength. However, his speed and quickness suffered a permanent setback due to the injury, but he had a good backup who was a very good athlete, but did not have the attributes of a running back.

During summer camp, whenever the kid would come to play QB, I rotated to tailback. I also remained at strong safety as part of our returning defensive secondary. There were four of us returning from the previous year, and it was a solid group of players. Our linebackers were mostly first-year starters, except for one guy who returned to anchor the group.

Another apparent strength surfacing at summer camp were our reserves, as well as a surprisingly talented incoming freshman team. Reserves have the talent to fill in when needed, and they were to complement exceptional players from our incoming freshman team. On the opposite side of the ball, we had decent talent and quite a few first-year starters with some uncertainty in a few key positions. All in all, there was good reason to be optimistic—running back was my natural position, and I was looking forward to proving it during the coming season.

One area of weakness was wide receiver. The position belonged to a first-year starter who played tight end the year before—he had good hands and ran good routes, but he was slow. In fact, he was so slow that I began to call him 'Slowmo', and the nickname stuck.

Our line was a young group of guys who were pieced together. Bobby, a member of my childhood crew, was on the team, and I never thought I would be playing varsity football with him. He went to Vigor, but he later transferred to Blount. He became our starting offense right guard, and it provided me a great deal of confidence to run the ball behind a guy I knew, and who was a childhood friend.

The summer training camp went well, and no serious injuries occurred. The kid made good progress at quarterback, and by the time our first game rolled around, Coach felt comfortable with him and me. I was what the coaches referred to as a 48-minute man. A 48-minute man was a player who started on offense and defense, and played on the special teams, as well. Since regulation time for a high school football game is twelve-minute quarters, a 48-minute man never leaves the field for the entire game. The two exceptions are at halftime, or an injury of some sort.

We opened the season with our regional rivals, Williamson High School. They beat us handily the year before, and they were returning their all state quarterback—we knew going into the game they would be hard to beat. Coach Harris simplified the game plan to match the inexperience of the kid who was starting his first ever game at QB. We weren't certain where our team stood at this point, since last year we failed miserably to meet preseason expectations. So, instead of predicting success, we opted to use caution as our ally. We weren't nearly as cocky or confident prior to the start of the season as the year before. That year, I felt the skepticism of the faculty and student body. Although they were still supportive, they didn't want to set themselves up for a letdown prior to the season opener. Personally, I was excited about the coming season, but I also had some mixed emotions. Life presented some new responsibilities that most seventeen-year-old student athletes will never have to worry about.

My girlfriend gave birth to our first born son on August 31, 1990.

I was happy to have a son, and I think I was too young to really understand the full responsibility of it all. I was still trying to fully understand who I was, and what I wanted in my future. It all occurred so fast, there was no practical way for me to prepare for it. Or, avoid it. It was a bit overwhelming!

The night my son was born, I was late getting to the hospital. We were in the middle of one of our occasional night practices which were held to give us a chance to practice our plays under artificial light at Prichard Stadium. Since the stadium was close to Mom's, she walked over to tell me Marilyn was on her way to the hospital. When I first heard the news I hesitated to leave practice, so Mom drove to the hospital without me. The prior week, I rushed Marilyn to the hospital due to false labor pains, and I assumed it was another one of those false alarms. When practice was over, I made my way to the hospital only to discover that Marilyn had already given birth. Although I missed the actual birth, I was happy to find out he was a perfectly healthy boy, and she was still alive.

I thanked God for watching over Marilyn, and giving us a healthy son. Having a child brought a whole element of self-awareness into my life, and I was more motivated than ever to make it on and off the football field. Once it started, the season consumed me—not too many things besides football and my family responsibilities really mattered to me, and I played every down as if my life depended on it—and, it did!

My crew members involved in 'the hustle' understood that during football season they wouldn't see me unless they were at the games. We continued our meetings as we did the previous year, but the hustle and hanging out would have to wait because I was committed to pursuing a football career.

I went into the season rated #8, overall, as a high school player in the State of Alabama, and #82 on the ESPN top 100 list—national. Soon, I received invitation letters from all the major colleges and universities across America. My personal rating as an athlete was four stars out of a possible five. The rating wasn't position specific—it was based on athleticism only. The truth was I played so many different positions in high school, it was impossible to rate me for a specific one. I could literally play almost any skilled position, and everyone who knew me was sold on the thought I was going to attend LSU in the fall. What they didn't know was I had not made any contact with LSU, so their thinking was premature.

Our season started with a close call at Williamson, but the game put us in first place in our region. It was a perfect set up for our next game against Greenville, a powerhouse in the 5A division. It was our first road game of the year, and highly anticipated by Blount fans. What made it even more interesting was Greenville was the team that eliminated us from the playoffs a couple of years previously.

We were confident after our first win, yet still uncertain about our team as a whole. During our win against Williamson, we controlled the ground game because I carried the ball over twenty-five times, and gained over 200 yards. But, against Greenville, we knew we would need to be effective in the passing game in order to win. When the big night arrived, our plan was to establish the passing game early. Unfortunately, the kid—our young QB—wasn't up to the task so we regrouped and returned to our bread and butter running game. By doing so, the game morphed into a defensive struggle. After a while, their offense began to methodically move the ball, and they struck pay dirt first.

After Greenville scored, we thought we would be in for a long night, but Coach Harris didn't panic because we had a lot of football left to play. He patiently stuck to his game plan and, before long, we answered Greenville's touchdown with one of our own. By halftime they struck again, and we went to the locker room down 14-7.

The guy who was a former Blount player volunteered his time to compile all of our team and individual statistics. During halftime, he told me I rushed for over 100 yards in the first quarter. In addition, I scored our only touchdown. My personal stats were in line with my expectations, but personal statistics weren't my concern. I wanted to win! This year was my last shot at winning the State Championship, and that was more important than anything!

We received the kickoff to start the second half, and drove the length of the field to score our second touchdown. The result of a ten-yard run, it tied the score. That meant two things—our game plan was still solid, and the momentum shifted as our confidence began to build.

Kickoff. Our defense took the field with a new level of confidence and, we stepped up and stopped their drive.

Punt. Next play we lined up over the ball, and I broke a seventy-yard, touchdown run. As my team in the Blount crowd celebrated, I jogged back to the sideline.

Unfortunately, when I looked at the field I noticed the flag, and the penalty was on us—the touchdown was called back. We couldn't overcome the penalty, and we were forced to punt—that's when the momentum started to shift, and the Greenville offense took over and began to move the ball well against our defense.

Their bread and butter was the option offense, and they were executing it perfectly.

Apparently, their coaching staff recognized the youth and inexperience of our linebackers, and their offense was starting to take advantage of our weakness. It was time for a change in defense of strategy, and Coach Carpenter called me over to tell me to go in as middle linebacker on the next defense series. I hadn't played linebacker since the first year of my childhood football career, and I had no practice in the position since then. But, I figured Coach Carpenter must've had confidence in my ability, or he wouldn't ask me to play the position for such an important situation. It took me a few snaps to get comfortable, but we held them to a field goal on that drive. So, I moved back to my offense and running back position, trailing 17-14 after the next kickoff. Soon after we took possession of the ball, I broke another long touchdown for sixty plus yards. Once again, in the midst of our celebrations, I found out there was another penalty against us. Sadly, these penalties would turn out to be the turning point of the game, and although we fought hard, we lost 24-14.

I finished the game with over 180 rushing yards and a touchdown, but the personal stats didn't make the loss hurt any less. I poured my heart out on the field on offense and defense, and we came up short. In fact, my emotions were so high that I cried as the clock wound down to zero. It was little consolation the players from the other team, as well as the kids from the stands, came up to me and praised my efforts. In particular, when the Greenville students and fans came onto the field to meet me, some of them were saying I was like a well-known running back from Colorado who wore jersey #1. For a running back he was small in stature, just like me, but he was a beast on the field. During my freshman year I wore jersey #41, but in my sophomore year I changed it to #1. So, the Greenville fans assumed I wore this number because I admired the Colorado football player. Yet, I was actually wearing it because of a guy named Carlos McMillan who was a teammate at Blount. When I met Carlos, he wore jersey #1. I admired his play, and I thought of him as a beast on the field. We grew to be good friends, but he was ineligible to play his senior year because of a late birthday. I liked the number, and decided to take it for myself.

I thanked everyone who came up to me, and continued to weep as I left the field and, when I made it to the team bus, my mother was there waiting for me. She noticed I was upset because of our loss, and she tried to gloss over it by telling me how well I played. It didn't work. Sometimes, when people try to cheer you up after emotional loss, it only makes things worse. I was sure we outplayed the other team, and we deserved to win. Yet, the reality was we lost.

I chose to deal with it by blaming our loss on home cooking, and poor officiating.

Excuses don't last long in sports, and our next game wasn't a repeat of the first. We continued to practice hard, and the effort paid off—we won our next four games. The next big test would be against our number one crosstown rival, Vigor High. Heading into the Vigor game, I hadn't beaten them at any level, starting with my freshman year. I was preparing for the game with a 0-3 overall record as a varsity player, and if I were ever going to turn it around, it had to be then!

Our opponent's football program was still very strong, but that year they lost more talent than they could replace. Instead of a perfect winning record, they came into our game with a record of 4-2. Two unusual losses. Conversely, we had a respectable record of 5-1 against good competition. I had the attitude of *if anyone can do it, why not us?* So, I went into the game with a level of confidence I never had before, and I felt we needed to execute and stick to the game plan in order to be successful.

One thing swaying the odds in their favor was the vast amount of players they had in uniform. It was lopsided in their favor because they were a larger 6A school compared to us at 5A. Nonetheless, I felt we had a more balanced team than they did, and it was really going to help that our quarterback had a few games under his belt. It was clear Coach Harris built up some confidence in his ability because he allowed him to throw more passes as the season went on.

The night of the big game arrived, and it started out well. I was pumped, and played with all of my heart, making some spectacular plays. But it wasn't enough to get the victory—we lost, despite my best efforts. Again, I was extremely upset after the game—that game was my last chance to win over Vigor, and we came up short. Even the loss to Greenville didn't hurt as badly. Then, from the field, I looked up at the crowd around me and, much to my surprise, I spotted my father. Ironically, it was the only high school game I played that he attended. And, even more ironic, he wasn't there because I was one of the featured players in the game—he was there because it was a big event for the city of Prichard. He tried to console me by telling me I played a good game and I had nothing to be ashamed of. What he didn't know was that it wasn't shame that fueled my emotions—it was passion. I was so passionate about the game that every time we lost it broke my heart.

There was always a big house party somewhere after our games, win or lose. Although I was devastated by the loss, I felt better as the night wore on—but, I didn't attend my high school house parties on this particular night. Robert John arranged for a limousine to pick me up from the school after our bus arrived. Marilyn was nowhere around because she was no longer a cheerleader. She missed cheerleader tryouts due to her pregnancy and, after giving birth to our son, she was at home that night caring for him. So, Robert John didn't think twice about arranging for some girls to be at the hotel when we arrived.

I figured I had two options available to me. One was to jump in the limo and drown my sorrows due to the agony of defeat, or to pick up and go home. I chose the former, showered and dressed, and headed out to the limo. When I approached the limo, Jeremy James met me. He was waiting at the school with the driver, and when the driver opened the door for me to get in I discovered the limo was filled with girls. I recognized most of them, but I never hung around with this particular crowd.

Jeremy informed me Robert rented the entire top floor at of one of the local hotels for a big party. Once we arrived, we made our way up to the room, and it was already packed with a mixture of girls and a few other dudes from the neighborhood. Most of the guys were drug dealers I knew from my past hustling activities, and Rich was there with his friend, Kenny Warmon. Kenny was a year younger than Rich and I, but I knew him well. He attended Blount for a brief time, and we hustled together a time or two in the past. We met a couple of years before on the street in Prichard and, one day, when I was visiting my cousin at his house, he told me he was Kenny's friend. Rich told me he heard some of the neighborhood boys were planning to kick Kenny's butt, and we needed to help Kenny get out of bad situation. We headed out to do whatever we needed to do and, when we arrived, Kenny was waiting alone. The boys who threatened to jump him didn't show up and, apparently, left the area. After that day, Kenny and I remained casual acquaintances.

That night after the game, Robert, Rich, Kenny, and I hung out together. We drank, smoked, and partied with the girls in the rooms Robert rented for the entire weekend— but, I went home the following morning. I stopped by Marilyn's house to check on her and the baby, and then I went to pick up Big Friendly. When I told him about the party that was still going on at the hotel, he wanted to check it out so he and I went back. Rich, Jeremy, and Kenny were still there, and Robert was still occupying the suite. All of them hung out together, worked the hustle all year round and, of the three, Jeremy was the only one who had enough sense to continue going to school to graduate. Soon, all of us hung out together on weekends after the games.

During the week, I wouldn't run with anyone in my circle of friends because I didn't want distractions before my upcoming games. It was always understood that nothing outside of family came before football and, although I didn't look for trouble, I landed in the middle of a number of street fights as the season progressed.

After the loss to Vigor, we picked up the pieces and went on a tear. We won all of our remaining regular-season games which included two 6A schools, Mary G, Montgomery, and Robert LeFlore. This put us in first place within our region, which meant we were set to host the first round of the playoffs.

Our first playoff game put us up against Atmore High School, a team we beat during the regular season, and we went into the game confident we would meet them again. After all, we vastly improved during the year, yet we also knew they were a solid opponent.

After we disposed of Atmore, we moved to the second round of the playoffs, and we learned we would travel to face our next formidable opponent. The first half of the game did not go our way, and we trailed at halftime, 21-7. During halftime, Coach Parker came to me and asked if I thought we had a chance to win. I've never been one to think about defeat, so I told him not to worry. I told him to just keep giving me the ball, and we were going to be just fine. As I think back to that statement, I was somewhat surprised I came up with such a positive response to his question. The truth was my confidence was shaken by our performance in the first half, and we had a major uphill battle on our hands if we were going to go home with the win.

And, I knew it.

Our opponent had two big time college recruits including the Hightower brothers, and there were many college scouts in the stands who came to see them play. But, we also had some very good players, and I was the leading high school rusher in the state of Alabama. I was also rated in the top five in the nation, and I figured our chances were good.

We won, 42-21, and headed into the state semi-finals hosting Valley High School. Valley had one loss on the year, and we had two, although we considered one loss due to poor officiating. It was going to be a great match up!

That time, Coach Parker came to me before the game to ask me if I thought we were going to win. I guess he thought I had a crystal ball, but the fact was I used simple logic. For me, any team having a loss on the record could be beaten, and we had a good enough team to beat anybody.

Coach Parker was the offensive coordinator, so he was responsible for developing the offense and game plan. The challenge was to find a balance between passing and running the ball against the defense of the opponent. That was his dilemma, and the reason he sought my input Although it was a different opponent, nothing changed and I responded to his question exactly as I had during the halftime of our previous playoff game. As it turned out, he did as I asked, and the outcome was the same. A resounding 24-14 win, and Blount High School's first ever trip to the Alabama State High School Championship Finals!

The moment the game ended the feeling was amazing! All of our hard work and dedication before and during the season paid off—we were finally where we wanted to be! Everyone associated with Blount High School was upbeat and high-spirited as we looked forward to the final and deciding game.

There is nothing more satisfying than the experience of a team coming together to reach a common goal. Whether it's an athletic, business, government, educational, or community effort, a bond that develops between people during the process of achievement is unbreakable. The school slogan, 'We are family' was now much more than words, and it had a special meaning to us. Earlier in the season, the meaning of the slogan was best demonstrated by my mother who was our official team mom. After one of our games at Prichard Stadium, all of my friends from the team stayed overnight at my mom's house. We went out after the game, and hooked up with Rich, Robert, and Jeremy, plus others. About fifteen of us crashed at my mom's home after our late night celebration, and the next morning my mom got up early, and cooked a big, hearty breakfast! We were still riding high, enjoying every minute of the team's success.

The week leading up to the championship game was mixed—we were hosting the game for the first time at Prichard Stadium, and it was the first of many 'firsts' for Blount High School. It was our first ever State Championship game, and the first time Prichard Stadium posted such a prestigious high school event. The town was swamped by media people and media hype. Blount was a virtual unknown as a football school at the state level, but our opponent, Homewood High, was a strong force in Alabama high school football. In fact, they had a few players highly recruited by some of the biggest college football programs across the country—including one of Homewood's top players, Robert Davis, who was a running back. Davis was the second leading rusher in the state behind me, and although the meeting promoted the game as a showdown between the two of us, I wasn't concerned about personal achievements. My main concern and personal focus was doing whatever it took to win the title. After all, I was living a dream!

Entering the game, I was the top rusher in the state and had amassed 2,828 yards rushing. Robert Davis logged 2100 plus yards rushing, and was a distant second place in the Alabama top five. Our stat man talked to me before the game and told me I had the number one position locked up. Then he reminded me I was 172 yards away from an incredible 3,000 yard season. I told him although it would be the icing on the cake, I didn't care about anything except winning the state title.

Finally, it was game day—time to put all the media hype behind us, and do our job as a team. The championship game was hard-fought, and we held on to win the state title 36-24—a fairytale ending to my high school football career! Not only did we win the Alabama State 5A High School Football Championship, but I set a new single-season Alabama State high school rushing and scoring record of 3,004 yards and 31 touchdowns! The class of 1990 was the catalyst that enabled our school to finally accomplish several of its long-term goals. My coaches, teammates, and I put the football program on the map with our first ever State Championship, and the entire class improved their test scores enough to earn our school accreditation.

I began to look ahead to the challenge of major college football, and the future of Blount High School was looking brighter than ever before!

Chapter 9
Signing with 'Bama

It was a season to remember! Blount High School Class 5A State Champs in football—a school once known for basketball as well as an exciting band, we were known as a legit football program. The championship had a little more sentimental value since I shared it with my childhood crew, and especially because Randal's mother finally approved him to play football. Bobby left the neighborhood, but returned in time to help when Leon wasn't a player—he was the bass drummer for our marching band, and the band was directly associated with our team. We regarded the championship as a group effort—cheerleaders, the band, faculty, parents in the Booster Club, team doctors, and our fans. All played parts in our becoming the team we were in the end.

Our principal was a hard-nosed man, a die hard football fan, and he supported our team the entire time he was at the school. Ever since the revamping, he witnessed the highs and the lows such as the times when we couldn't afford new jerseys for the game. The previous season, we wore mix-matched helmets and, for most games, we painted numbers on our jerseys so fans, refs, and coaches could see us. It's an understatement to say a few things needed to be done. But, through it all, we managed to pull together and win—and, with the championship under our belts, things were going to change. When a school wins a championship, the state gives it bonus money for its athletic program. Regretfully, I was a senior and wouldn't be there the following season to enjoy the fruits of our labor, but I was happy to be a part of the experience.

Due to our win, the atmosphere at the school was upbeat and high spirited as it was with the entire community. The Mayor of Prichard held a parade complete with a motorcade and our marching band. We ended up at City Hall where the Mayor addressed our team, introducing each one of us as we walked across the stage. We shook hands and posed for photos, and there was little doubt it was a good day for Blount. Coach Harris won Coach of the Year, and I was named Player of the Year for Class 5A, plus runner up for Mr. Football for the State of Alabama. Throughout the season, I won Player of the Week on several occasions—a favorable statistic when it was open season for recruiting. Letters poured in from major universities, and everyone who knew me was aware of how much I wanted to play for LSU. It scouted and recruited me to attend the university in the fall under Head Coach, Curly Hallman, but I wasn't sure—LSU had a decent program, but it wasn't a powerhouse.

I needed to see what else what out there.

East and West Coast schools called Coach Harris about me, and he relayed the messages as they came in. It got to the point of my telling Coach the only schools I was interested in were schools in the Southeastern Conference (SEC). We talked about it, and he thought it would be good if I considered historically black colleges and universities

(HBCU). He attended an HBCU, Alabama State University, where he played quarterback—in fact, the majority of our coaching staff attended HBCUs and, since Blount was an all-black high school, I decided I should visit at least one. At the time, we were only allowed five official visits to different schools and because I agreed with Coach to visit an HBCU, I had only four official visits to 1A schools—HBCUs were 1AA schools.

Weeks after football season was over, indoor track and field began. We had already won the Indoor and Outdoor Championships the past two years, and our senior class was going for the repeat. It was unfortunate the Indoor State Championship Track Meet was on one of the weekends during the time we were allowed our official visits. So, that left me with only 3 official visits. I could use them in a couple of different ways—I could use all three visits with one school, or I could mix them up. I strongly considered taking all three visits to LSU, but decided against it.

National Signing Day was February 1, and that meant I had the entire month of January to decide what school to attend in the fall. My ACT scores weren't high enough to qualify for a full athletic scholarship even though I took qualifying courses. I was good in the classroom department, so all I had to do was pass the ACT to avoid becoming a Proposition 48 player—a scholarship player who didn't qualify to participate in athletics for a whole year until he or she cleared academic standards. Each school carried one of these athletes each year.

The required ACT score at that time was 18, and the first time I took it I scored a 16. Unfortunately, I took the test for granted, and thought I could pass it without studying—that was during the time of my expulsion during the spring of my junior year. It didn't help that I was hustling and hanging out with Da Fellas. The ACT consisted of math, social studies, science, and language arts, and I passed science and social studies with flying colors. Not so with math and language arts. I admit it—I was rusty, and I hadn't taken math since my sophomore year. Language Arts wasn't a strong suit for me because in my home environment speaking correctly wasn't a top priority. We spoke slang, and in sentence fragments laced with profanity. Luckily, colleges decided to recruit me in spite of my low scores, and they took their chances by offering me scholarships while hoping I would pass the ACT.

Weeks after football season ended and as track season began, I picked up with Rich, Jeremy, and Kenny but hanging out with them didn't change the fact I had a three month old son. Diapers. Formula. Medical bills! All expensive, and I realized there was only one solution—I had to return to my entrepreneurial roots and make money. Since I stopped driving the van and didn't have a hustle during the football season, I figured the heat around me died down. But, winning the State Championship as well as the accolades and media coverage was a double-edged sword. I was a local super star. Everyone in Prichard knew who I was. No way I could hustle around Prichard without being noticed by someone.

I had to be discreet. Make money and get out. Change locations. I talked to one of my crew, and he told me he knew a spot on the other side of town where money was being made. His girlfriend had two older brothers who hustled in that area, and my establishing a business in their neighborhood was cool with them. So, my new hustle was near Williamson High School—one of our toughest opponents in all sports, and it was a mirror image of my school—all black with a good athletic program. The girl's track team dominated, and one of my junior high friends led the team. Not many knew me, but I had a reputation. Two brothers of a friend of mine knew the project life well, but they were too young to command respect in the hustle. However, when the two older guys recognized me in their house, they welcomed me with open arms.

A good set up for me.

During that time, I struck up a relationship with a girl who ran track for Williamson. She had a crush on me from the previous track season, and she flirted with me every time she got a chance. I tried to hide my dealing from her because I didn't want her to run her mouth about what I had going on, but she was cool with everything and we were friends from then on.

Indoor track season went well. Blount won the title for the boys, and the Williamson girls won, too. The good thing about indoor track was there weren't any meets before the state title meets. We practiced for a few weeks, and then went to Montgomery—mainly because it was the only place in the state with an indoor track. Plus, since the state track meet was the third weekend in January, I could use three of my official visits before the meet.

I decided to take my HBCU visit during the holiday break to get it out of the way—Southern University in Baton Rouge, Louisiana, the same city as LSU. Coach Harris set it up with the recruiting coach, and he picked me up at school in a fifteen-passenger van. On our way to Baton Rouge we picked up a few more guys, stopped in New Orleans for a quick dinner, then it was on to our final destination.

Overall, the trip was good—but, I was set to return in a few weeks to visit LSU. I told Coach I wasn't leaving the SEC and I had only three visits left, so I narrowed the schools down to three—Alabama, Auburn, and LSU. My interest in LSU was a given—I was sold on it when I made out my schedule, and I wanted to visit Auburn and Alabama only because I was born in Alabama.

First, Auburn. The university had a decent football program, but it wasn't on my radar. Nonetheless, I drove up to Auburn with Mom and her husband. When we arrived, I met up with a guy who was my escort for the tour, and it turned out I played against him when I was a sophomore. I'm not sure what Auburn did to him, but he didn't have too many positive things to say about the school, or its coach. Mom and her husband met with the other coaches, and all of us linked up for dinner at the coach's house. By the time we made it back there, I was too drunk to speak or eat— other than that, it was a smooth trip. Mom, though, was still sold on my attending LSU since I didn't commit while I was at Auburn.

Second, the University of Alabama. I visited the campus the previous year with Coach Harris and a few other players—then, we only attended the game and went home. This time was different—an official visit. When we arrived, the defensive line coach met us—he was responsible for recruiting the Southern area of Alabama. Then we met with the running back coach, and he reminded me of one of my coaches at Blount. They introduced us to our escorts, a guy and girl. He was a player on the team, and she was a 'Bama Belle. 'Bama Belles' was a group of girls who volunteered to help recruits during their visits.

At the time, Gene Stallings was the head coach. We met for dinner at the Sheraton Hotel which was a 5-star hotel and restaurant located on the campus. Then we checked into our rooms and settled in. I was lucky—there were other recruits visiting that same weekend, and I knew one of them from my visit to Auburn. He was a local player from Tuscaloosa—a highly recruited linebacker—and he knew all along he would attend Alabama. But, there was one thing that really caught my attention—on our way to the table, we passed a glass encasement protecting a Crimson #1 Alabama Jersey with my name on it! I was stunned, but I confess I couldn't take my eyes off it!

I wasn't an Alabama fan then, I really didn't know anything about Coach Stallings, and my first impression was he reminded me of John Wayne. The way he spoke. His body language. He seemed a nice man, and our dinner was peaceful and we enjoyed ourselves. As recruits, we learned about the program, and its coaching staff. Coaches and people who mattered in the program tried to persuade us to sign with their school, but I wasn't ready to commit. So far, I was impressed, but I wasn't ready to let go of my dream to attend LSU.

Then it was time for a night on the town.

After dinner with the coaches and staff, we went to the athletic dorm to hang out with a few other players, and the atmosphere was pleasant—the way the players interacted made me think of my old team at Blount. There was a party on campus they were planning to attend, so we had a few drinks and played a few games of spades while a few of the other guys got dressed.

We went to the party as a team—that impressed me. And, there were a couple of players on the team from Prichard who played for Vigor. I played against them in high school, but really never hung out with them. But, this night all of us were part of the same unit. When I talked to them they told me I should play with them because they were going to win the National Championship the following year. I believed 'em because they were on the Vigor team that won the National High School Championship—they understand the value of a team. They also spoke highly of the program and the coaching staff.

All in all, the party went well that night, and I also saw Big Friendly's sister—she was a student at Alabama. She knew me because I spent the night at her mother's house a few times when she was home on break. It was nice to see a familiar face from home, so I decided to hang out with her and her friends since she was like family. Sometime during our conversation, she advised it would be a good idea for me to accept the scholarship offer from Alabama. *But, what about LSU?* Truth was my visit to Alabama wasn't anything like I expected—all the childhood stigmas made me think Alabama was a racist university—but, after spending time there, any thoughts of racial bias were erased. I had a different opinion after listening to all the black kids tell me how great the school was. I was totally caught off guard! At that point, I was sold on Alabama. I was ready to commit, but with a few reservations. However—I still had to visit LSU.

The Indoor State Championship Track Meet was business as usual. Blount won the Championship for 5A boys, and Williamson won for 5A girls. I hung out with old friends, and both teams stayed overnight in adjacent hotels. I took a few of the Da Fellas with me, and we had a great time as I knew we would. The best part was we returned home with the win! Yes, it was a great feeling, but the truth was no one really cared. There was never any fanfare surrounding the track team no matter how many championships we won. Never a parade. Never kudos for a job well done. We received rings, and the ceremonies were at the school—and, the only way we got rings was if we won the indoor and outdoor track titles.

When I got home it was back to my routine, and

I returned to my hustle in the RV Projects. With a week before my visit to LSU, a friend and I were at a girl's house one day when one of her friends stopped by. When I saw her face, I instantly remembered her from our first encounter—she was one of the girls walking the street behind Vigor. The day our BBV war started. I brought our first meeting to her attention, and she remembered. She said one of those dudes was her boyfriend at the time, but they were no longer together. Back then, I was only seventeen, and she was fifteen. We chatted for a couple of minutes, and the conversation ended with my requesting her phone number.

But, I didn't call right away.

****

I was on my way to visit LSU with Mom's husband, Mom, and me. I was amped for it was the most anticipated visit of all because, unlike Southern, Auburn, and Alabama, I had high expectations for LSU. So far, Alabama made the best impression on me, but Mom was still convinced LSU was where I wanted to be.

We arrived in Baton Rouge, and I was somewhat familiar with the city from my visit to Southern a few weeks prior. The LSU campus was quite different from Southern's, and the man responsible for recruiting my district coached wide receivers. We met him on campus and it was the same routine as Auburn and Alabama—check in at the hotel, and dinner with the head coach and parents. My escort and host was from Mobile, and played for John LeFlore High School. Then, he played free safety for LSU. I recalled his being a good player at LeFlore even though he was two years ahead of me. He liked it at LSU, but had mixed feelings at times.

Strange. During my visit, I sensed dissension between the players, and they didn't seem to have the family unit feel I experienced at Alabama. I wasn't ready to give up my heart, however—it was still with LSU.

We went to the athletic dorm and met with a few players. The reception wasn't as welcoming as I would have liked, and most of the players weren't around. I did have an interesting conversation with a fella who was a wide receiver for the team. I recognized him—his jersey was #1, and he was from Florida. He, too, wasn't happy about the way things were going with him at LSU. He said one thing I'll never forget—*he wished he would have stayed within his home state.*

Again, after the obligatory dinner, we partied. I was pretty surprised when I recognized Shaquille O'Neil as the DJ! I had an opportunity to meet him, and he seemed to be a cool guy.

The night ended on a good note.

After touring the campus and meeting the coaches, we returned home. Mom maintained her staunch position, and she was still set on my attending LSU. She was even more convinced after our visit. But her passion for LSU didn't matter—after all the visits, my heart was with Alabama.

****

The weeks leading up to National Signing Day, schools made their final pushes to build their teams. Gene Stallings came to Prichard, and all four schools offered me a scholarship pending my ACT score. I was confident I would pass because I studied between track, hustling, and visiting schools. I even went so far as to have a study partner—he planned on going to college, as well.

My study partner's neighborhood was gang affiliated—the GDs. His cousin was in one and, once in a while, he'd come by the house when I was there. I was consistently asked to become a member and, finally, I decided to accept the offer while holding claim to my Crip set. I met some Crips in Mobile, and I often visited their neighborhood to party. A guy named Tyrese Morris lived in a Crip neighborhood in West Mobile and, when he transferred to Blount during our junior year, I hung with him. One thing I did have in common with the GDs was both gangs were at war with BBV.

The week leading into signing day, I made the call to LSU and committed. The coach was set for me to sign my Letter of Intent on signing day—this stemming from the advice of my mother. I was sure I made the right decision, but later that evening I received a phone call from Larry Kirksey, the running back coach at the University of Alabama.

It was a long conversation.

A very long conversation.

The short story is I changed my commitment, and decided Alabama was the best fit for me and my family. After I explained it to Mom she agreed with me, and supported my decision. Of course, there was a lot of media hype—I held a press conference at the Blount High School library, and publicly announced my plans to attend the University of Alabama in the fall. Many people were shocked by the best and biggest decision of my life, and it set the course of my future.

Later that spring, I passed the ACT without a hitch. I was academically eligible to receive the full scholarship, and all I had to do was finish high school, pass the exit exams, and receive a diploma. After all the recruiting trips and signing my intent to go to the University of Alabama, I continued to hustle, and I met up with a girl I knew from before—she told of her plans to move north, so we decided to hang out the night before her leaving. Cheap wine. Sex. Then, we went our separate ways.

Pregnant.

I was in shock. I asked the usual questions—*are you sure? Is it mine? How could it happen after only one encounter?*

She moved back to Mobile so her parents could help her with the pregnancy. I was seventeen, and had a child the previous August—now, the possibility of another. By this time, I was deep in the hustle and, after the news, I figured there was no way for me to get out of the game. *How was I going to go to college with two kids? How could I provide for them? Marilyn was still my girlfriend—how would I break the news to her? What about my mother? How was I going to explain this?*

I decided to keep the matter to myself.

When she returned home, I spent more time on her end of town. I was still in school at Blount, so I would spend the night at her house, get up for school, meet Marilyn, take her to school, go to track practice, drop Marilyn off at work, see my son, and hustle.

I needed some sleep!

Chapter 10
College Bound

I t seemed as if after I signed with Alabama things happened quickly. I was no longer interested in being a part of the track team—before signing, I always kept track as a college option mainly because my brother earned a track scholarship. I figured if I didn't make it playing football, I could fall back on track. But after I signed, I no longer needed track. The result? I took it for granted. I stopped training and showing up for meets. Before then, the track coach and I had a pretty good relationship—but, we grew distant because of my poor choices. Unfortunately, it happened at the time of the preliminaries for the State Track Meet to determine which competitor would participate in each event. The rule was if I didn't qualify, I wouldn't be allowed to make the trip. Previously, I always qualified in two field events—the long jump and triple jump. However, during my senior year, I decided I would only participate in the long jump, a skill I learned from my brother at a young age. To qualify for State, I had to finish in the top three. I was also on two relay teams—I ran as anchor leg on the 4 x 100 meter, and the third leg of the 4 x 400, plus the open 100 meters.

As usual, the night before the qualifying meet, Coach gave us a long speech in which he stated if we didn't show up on time for the meet the next day or missed our event, we were out of luck. No traveling with the team. Apparently, that didn't sink in with me. That same night I hung out with my friends, taking the meet for granted. I missed the long jump event, and it was the only individual event for which I could qualify. I wasn't one of the top three fastest in the 100 meters, and Coach wouldn't allow me to participate on the relay teams.

The 4 x 400 was the last event of the day, and I knew it would be my ticket to State, but Coach had other plans. He refused to allow me to run on the relay teams since I missed the long jump, and showed up late. So, for the first time in my track career, I didn't qualify to travel with the track team to the State championship meet. Even though I didn't have a need to participate in track and field, I was still disappointed by Coach's decision. All of Da Fellas were going, and we always looked forward to an all expense paid trip out of town on the school board's tab—hotel rooms, full course meals, and girls. Not to mention we always won the State Indoor and Outdoor Championships. Life without track and field made things worse—instead of having a positive outlet in my life, I was involved in more delinquent behavior. I started hanging out on the blocks, became more involved in street life, and continued relationships with shady characters.

I already accepted my scholarship to the University of Alabama, but I still had work to do to qualify. This was during the early days of Proposition 48 when a certain ACT score was required to qualify and receive a scholarship. I already qualified, and the first time I took the test I scored a 16. The minimum requirement was a 18. But, I took it in the middle of football season, early on a Saturday morning after a Friday night football game. Every Friday night we would go to our local McDonald's, and hang out in the parking lot full of high school students. It was more like a block party than anything else. Students from three high schools—Vigor, Blount and LeFlore—were there. Not many were of legal drinking age, but there was always an abundant supply of alcohol and drugs.

I can't lie. I was one of the participants. Another poor choice—but, the drinking and smoking didn't work for me the next morning when I had to report to Bishop State Community College no later than eight o'clock. I made it there on time because I promised my mother I would, and I spent the night with the mother of my second child. Yes, I made it on time, barely keeping my eyes open. I was too tired to concentrate, and I got to a point where I couldn't read the booklet.

I had a hangover and a headache.

On Saturdays, I usually stayed inside the house recovering from the game the night before, and wracking my brain to take a test wasn't in the game plan. I was ill-prepared, and I proceeded through the test by marking answers without looking at the questions—a practice that lead to my score of 15. The second time around, though, things were different. I was under pressure to perform, and that's how I liked it—performing under pressure is when I did my best work. In order for me to accept my scholarship, I had to have at least an 18, and I only had two more chances left before the end of the school year. I vowed I would qualify the second time around because I didn't want to find myself in a do-or-die situation. So, I decided to attend tutoring sessions at Bishop State. I went two hours a day, three days a week for six to eight weeks. It was cool, and I learned enough to easily pass the test. My second effort garnered a score of 25—a ten-point swing. That swing was so great, the administrators at the main test office didn't believe I was able capable of making such considerable improvement. If they knew about the behind the scenes tutoring, they would have understood.

The night before I took the second test there wasn't a game—no hanging out until two or three in the morning, no drugs or alcohol, and I had a tutor. I crashed early the night before, got up early, ate a good breakfast, and was alert for the entire exam. That made all the difference in the world!

Too bad none of it mattered.

Administration placed me under investigation, voided my test score, and forced me to retake the test. They justified their decision and actions by saying my grade point average and previous score didn't support such a high score. Interestingly, another of my teammates went through the same thing, so it didn't make me feel as though they were picking on me. It was ironic—I did everything I could to avoid the do-or-die situation, and yet I found myself there anyway. At least the third time around, I was confident I would pass because I didn't have a hangover.

The third time, I went through the same ritual as the second test. But it was a 360 degree turnaround from the first test—unlike the first test, I marked answers I knew were wrong even though I knew the right answer. I wanted to dumb myself down to score only enough to qualify. When the results came back, I was very happy to see I scored a 19. That score satisfied everybody—me, the university, and the ACT administration.

****

Things were starting to take shape. At this point, my future and college were real, and I knew things could be better for me if I were in a different environment. Everything good I had going on didn't change my circumstances, or where I lived.

Graduation excitement mounted. I had a son who was six months old, as well as a girlfriend who was two months pregnant—all before graduating high school. Being a dad meant I had to find some way to provide for them, and I couldn't ask my mother to take on my responsibility. With no football, minimal track, and the ACT behind me, I didn't have anything happening. I considered getting a job, but decided against it. Since I was out on the block, getting back in the street game made sense, but my face was too recognizable for Prichard—the only way I could make it work was by working on my girlfriend's end of town. That way, I would be out of the way.

It worked, too—for a few weeks. I quickly hustled a few grand—hustling on that end of town, and hanging out and partying on the Prichard end provided what I needed. Plus, I was trying to workout and stay in shape. Only one thing kept my mind on football—selection to play in the Alabama-Mississippi High School All-Star Game after school was out for the summer. It was a big honor for a local kid in the Mobile area because we played in Mobile's Ladd-Pebbles Stadium. The game was bittersweet—I played my last high school game with the best of the best from Alabama and Mississippi with future NFL players on both teams.

From then on, life warped from slow motion to a full plate. Between hustling on the block, training for the game, as well as trying to finish high school, the end of the school year was near. Some students were glad, and some felt the pressure of life after high school. The real world. Me? I looked forward to playing football at the University of Alabama. Making money wasn't a real serious concern for me because I knew I would always be able to get my hands on it.

I was entrenched in the drug trade.

One of the most popular things of my senior year was senior skip day—a day when all seniors were excused from class. It was an unwritten rule and such a tradition that administration, teachers, and coaches knew about it—they remembered their own senior-skip days! On our senior skip day, we planned a trip to Pensacola Beach, Florida. These trips happened around the same time for all of Mobile County Schools and, this particular year, we were there at the same time with schools from crosstown—Vigor, Blount and LeFlore. In those days, there was always a section of the beach considered the Black section, and that's where we ended up.

There was a huge crowd at the beach that day—me, Da Fellas, and our girls included. Marilyn and I were still together, our son was eight months old, and Grandma took over babysitting duties while we took our trip. The beach wasn't new to me, but, on that day, it seemed as if there were more people than usual. Everything was going fine— we hung out, had a good time, and coolers were stuffed with alcoholic beverages and good weed.

I was training for the All-Star game, so I decided not to drink or smoke anything. I was good with being there, hanging with Da Fellas and my son's mother. It was only a matter of time—and, it never fails—that a large crowd of unruly, drunk and high teenagers instigated a massive fight. When I say massive, I mean over 100-200 people. Guns. Shots. Girls and guys ran wild and the cops showed up on the scene, closing the entire beach. This fight was so out of control, it aired on all the local channels' ten o'clock news—it was known that high school students from the Mobile County School System were responsible for all the ruckus. After that day, Florida officials monitored the amount of traffic with a Mobile tag entering the beach. I know because we tried to visit the beach a few weeks later, and they refused us because of our Mobile tag.

The beach outing was just one of the events on my list of things to do—I didn't make it to the senior picnic because I was training for the All-Star Game. I got up each morning and ran three miles in the neighborhood, showered, then headed to school to catch up with Da Fellas—I wanted to hang out with them and attend mandatory classes. By then, I was going to school to use the weight room since I already fulfilled the requirements to graduate. After school, I packed up and took off for Mayesville so I could hustle on the block—it was a routine that worked well for me. I had two girlfriends on separate ends of town—the girl I loved already gave birth to my oldest son, and the girl I needed was pregnant with my oldest daughter.

In the meantime, we were planning our end of the year senior class party—the party of the year. Most of our parties were at my mother's house since her house was next to Prichard Stadium, and there was a big field surrounding it. Da Fellas were used to staying at Mom's after games and parties, and they knew we were going to wake up Saturday morning to a big country breakfast—the same as years previous. They always looked forward to it because she treated them like her own. That year, however, we decided to hold our senior class party at another one of our teammates' mom's house. Since we had an ongoing beef with the BBV, we thought it best to host it in a more low-key environment. Well, we should have known—there was no such thing as Da Fellas having a low-key party in Prichard. At one point, we thought we could hang out without bringing our guns—an idea that was a fool's folly. The last party ended with a gun blast, and we figured if we didn't allow guns we might end the night on a good note. The only thing was we couldn't agree. In the end, however, we couldn't afford being caught ill-prepared at a party without packing heat.

Guns it was.

We planned the party, and everything was going well until some of the BBV's showed up with guns blazing— turned out they followed one of Da Fellas to the party house. We were having a great time until gunshots rang out, and I knew in that second we made the right decision to bring our weapons.

By this time, we were in a full-blown, out-and-out war. More gunshots. People screaming. Bullets flying. The feud was going on for a few years by that point—they shot a couple of our guys, and a few guys from their side were hit. This time, another one of their guys was shot—so, once again, one of our parties ended in gunfire.

On the Monday following graduation and the party, I worked out and headed to see my son because his mom lived two blocks up the road from my mom's house. When I pulled into Mom's yard, I noticed she was home from work. She met me at the door, telling me the police came by the house with a warrant for my arrest. My first thought was that someone snitched about my drug activity on the other side of town. Or, maybe I sold to an undercover cop. Maybe it was a secret indictment. None of those—it was from the night of the party. Mom said the officer told her I should be out of detention the same day. The timing of my arrest was terrible—and, at that time, the popularity of prosecuting a youth as an adult was rising.

While waiting to see the judge, I had to remain in detention for up to three weeks before he was available. There was no way—the All-Star Game was the next weekend, and I had to be out of the city. Mom called some of the Alabama folks as well as Coach Harris to inform them of the situation. Coach Harris was the Head Coach of the All-Star team, as well as the 5A Coach of the Year. He visited me at the detention center to see if he could help— but there wasn't anything anyone could do.

While at the detention center, my thoughts jockeyed for position and, for the first time, there was a serious possibility I could lose everything. Everything. I wasn't sure if Alabama would honor my football scholarship if I couldn't get out of detention, and I really wanted to play in that All-Star Game. I needed to play in that game. During previous years it was different because we played football during the fall, and I focused on football—no outside activity. No hustling, getting involved in fights, or shootouts. But, my situation was different because after signing Alabama, football was number one from then on.

I developed a routine from the previous years, but didn't realize I couldn't continuing doing things the same as I did in the past. It took detention for me to understand I really needed to make a change—and, the only way to do that was to change my environment. While on lockdown, I decided to ask Mom if there were anyone in our family, or friends, with whom I could spend time away from Prichard and Mobile.

Days passed, and I was still locked down not knowing my circumstances. I didn't like the fact my good friend and one of Da Fellas was locked down for a shooting that I witnessed him commit. But, it was good to have someone I could talk to. He was like a brother to me, and he was there

because one day after school a local guy broke into his car
to steal dope. When we discovered the break-in we went
through Grant's Circle, a neighborhood next to the school,
and folks there told us who broke into the car. They also
told us they had the dope. We walked back to the school,
hopped in one of Da Fella's truck with our guns, and went
looking for the dude who broke into his car. No questions
asked—my friend pulled out his gun, shot him on the spot,
and we sped off.

He turned himself in the following day.

The shooting was a month or so before our party and,
since he was in detention for at least a month, he schooled
me on the rules—written and unwritten. For the most
part, detention was pretty laid back—a jungle filled with
all sorts of characters. Even though we were in the same
place, my friend and I didn't fit in with this crowd. He was
the starting middle linebacker for our state championship
winning football team, and when scholarship offers poured
in, he decided on Alabama State University. He was a smart
kid with a bright future, but, once again, the environment
of Prichard, Alabama was about sucking the potential
out of a good kid who had a shot to lead a successful life.
Fortunately, God found favor in his life, and his sentence
was to attend a ninety-day boot camp which allowed him
to graduate.

My friend's life story is similar to mine, and while we
were in detention we encouraged each other to stay positive.
He had to keep me calm because I was so uncertain—I
didn't know how long I would be there, or if I would play
in the game. I had one child, and one on the way. Would
I lose my scholarship? I didn't know, and my life was up in
the air. My friend always broke everything down into the
worst case scenario saying at the end, "You're going to be

alright, though." Still, no matter his words, time ticked by and I grew impatient. The closer it got to Friday, the more concerned I got because if I didn't get out for the weekend I couldn't play in the game—we had to report by eight o'clock Monday morning.

Friday came and went.

For a brief moment, I thought I was going crazy. Saturday was the longest day of my entire life, and it was easy to see a significant difference between me and my friend. Compared to seventy-five percent of the boys locked up with us, most of them had already dropped out of school, frequently returned to detention, and didn't have any future plans or goals. They weren't well-groomed, and they were truly bad kids. I knew we were bad, but they were a different type of bad.

I tried to sleep as many hours as I could, but all I could do was lay there and stare at the ceiling. I rewound the night of the party in my head, thinking about what I could have done differently. First, we should have left our guns at home. On the other hand, if I didn't have my gun with me I might be dead. Again, I considered how I needed to change.

My only outside communication was with my mother, and she hired an attorney for me. When I spoke with her on Saturday, she informed me the lawyer was coming to see me on Monday morning. That news offered a little relief because, at least, I would know what I was facing. Later that night, a guard came around with religious material about church service that would take place the following day. Having something to look forward to the next day help a bit, and my friend told me bits and pieces about the service, but without much detail. I vividly recall attending that service and reciting a prayers such as, "If you get me out of this mess, I promise I won't do it again!" I hoped God listened.

The gentleman who came in to minister to us was older Caucasian man and he discussed God, as well as our needing to pray and believe in Him. So, I said my prayers, and asked God to get me out, let me play in the game, and keep my scholarship. Maybe more. It felt good to participate in the service—it wasn't mandatory, so the crowd was very small, and my personal inspiration was looking forward to my lawyer coming.

I awakened bright and early Monday morning, full of anticipation. But, before my thoughts consumed me, the guards told me to pack my things—which wasn't much—and step to the door. I went to a large room monitored by a couple of guards who encouraged me by telling me to take it easy. Positive, big brother advice. It was several minutes before another door opened, and on the other side were my mother and my lawyer. Somehow, God worked it out so I was on the early docket with the presiding judge. With my being a juvenile, I didn't even have to be in court. My Mom signed for the bond, and put her house up as collateral. The early docket began at six thirty in the morning, and my name was near the top of the list. By the time it was all said and done, it was close to eight-thirty.

I was already late.

Check-in was at the University of South Alabama campus, and even though I didn't actually arrive until after nine, check-in was still in full swing—I wasn't even the last person to arrive, and my anxiety was for nothing! I learned a valuable lesson that things are never as bad as they seem.

After my incarceration, everything happened right on time. One of my high school teammates, best friend, and a Da Fella also made the team. He was an offensive lineman, and we were roommates for the week. He was excited to see me when

I came into the room, and he said he didn't doubt my playing in the game. I told him whatever he knew, I wished he would have told me a few days ago—it would have saved me a lot of stress! He said, "C'mon, man—we in Alabama, and you signed with Alabama. You know 'Bama folk were going to get you out of there." I confided my prayers, and he told me God used those 'Bama folks to get me out. It made sense.

A few minutes later, Coach Harris stopped by, and he never said a thing about my being in the detention center. He only came by the dorm to check on us. I guess since he was the Head Coach, it was his responsibility to make sure we were where we were supposed to be. Still, Coach Harris wouldn't have done it any other way. He also gave us a practice schedule, and one thing that disappointed me was it was the first year we weren't to wear our high school helmets.

We wore plain white, cheap-looking helmets.

Our first day, as soon as we ate lunch, we had to report to the practice field. Somewhere between check in and after practice, Big Friendly had already set up one of Da Fellas to bring a few cases of beer to our dorm room and, by the time I made it back there, he had four or five lineman in the room getting hammered. They offered me beer, and I declined. Friendly told them I was cool, and I just had a lot on my mind from the week before, his words designed to make certain I was accepted by my teammates.

After practice, I thought our team was good, but not that good. We needed more offense, but our defense played well. I mentioned it to one of the guys who was in the room, and he said, "Don't worry—we have a guy named David Palmer who is coming tomorrow." Palmer was Alabama's Mr. Football for that year—I recognized his name from the paper, but I didn't see him play. Another guy was to arrive, as well. They arrived early and ate lunch with us, but I didn't get to meet them because I worried about what I had going on off the field. One thing about football—it was always therapy for me. When on the field, it were as if no one could touch me, and I was much more relaxed.

When David and Vint showed up, I was more confident about winning the game. David and I introduced ourselves during warm-ups, and we practiced punts and kicks. We hit it off from that day, realizing we were similar—we loved football, had children, and we already signed with Alabama. And, it wasn't long before we befriended Damien Jefferies—all of us became friends over the next few days.

From that first night we had the guys come back to our dorm room, and a few boys from Mississippi started coming by to see if they could buy some beer from us. Friendly and I called our homeboys and placed the order, but the ongoing traffic to and from our dorm room raised suspicion and Coach Harris got wind of what we were doing. Whoever ratted us out said it was Big Friendly, not me, and Coach stormed into our room and cussed Friendly out. He said he had half a mind to make him get up and run at eleven o'clock—he eventually calmed down, however, and left our room. His rant must not have made much of an impression on us, because we still had a good time that night.

By the end of the week, David and I cemented our friendship. We introduced our children's mothers, and they, too, became good friends. During that time we vowed to become roommates when we arrived on campus in the fall—but only if everything worked out with my situation. David was from Birmingham, so when game day arrived, many of his family and friends traveled to see him play. His mother came, and we introduced our mothers and, by then, we were like family.

The week's events ended in victory, and we won the game even though we were a two-touchdown underdog—

it was supposed to be Mississippi's year since they never won an All Star game. David and I had a good game, and I scored the game go-ahead touchdown while David made two big catches on the game-winning drive. Everyone was ecstatic!

After the game, I didn't return to detention. Instead, Mom packed all of my stuff and sent me to Fort Stewart, Georgia to stay with my sister for the whole summer until the court case was solved. By then, my sister was pregnant and her husband was in the military. So, I loaded up the Escort, returning only for court dates. While there, I did all of my training on the military base with two guys from Detroit who were there for the summer to visit their uncles. I still wasn't in the clear from my court case, and it weighed heavily on me while I was in Georgia. It helped to get up early and run the P. T. training with my brother-in-law and other army guys before going to stay with my sister on the military base.

Previously, joining the military wasn't a consideration, but with my situation it became a serious option. Before my going to Georgia, the last time I stayed away from Prichard longer that a week or weekend was when I had to stay the summer with my sister in California when I was a budding teenager. The military always provided the brotherhood, family feel which was similar to football—a group of individuals working hard toward a common goal—and when I was on the football field, there was a sense of war. The concepts are the same, except the military could be life, death, do or die—all aspects of the military I didn't like. In many ways, the military was similar to living in Prichard—but, my idea was to get out and not live that way.

While in Georgia, time with my sister and being away from Prichard allowed me to develop a new outlook on life. I wanted to make a change. I wanted to do things differently. I craved positivity. My Army workout buddies offered words of encouragement each day, treating me like one of them. While I was there, I began to experience a new way of living—and it was definitely better than living in Prichard!

I returned to Mobile for court dates once a month, and I made the trip three times. I arrived at Mom's late at night, sneaked into town, and went to court the following day. As soon as I left the courtroom, I headed to Georgia because Mom didn't want me to be in Prichard one second more than I needed to be. Finally, the court dismissed my case because there were no witnesses nor enough evidence to prosecute.

Georgia was good for me—after living there for three months, I told my mother I didn't ever want to return to Prichard. I saved up money from when I was hustling on the blocks before I caught the attempted murder case. Without running track, I had more time to hustle than I did in previous years and, between taking care of my son and the one I had on the way, I still managed to save over twenty five thousand dollars. I gave my sister a couple of grand for letting me stay with her for those two months— not nearly enough for what I gained.

****

From the time David and I met, we stayed in constant communication. My Mom talked to his mom, and my son's mom stayed in touch with his kids' mom. Our connection seemed a natural fit—and, even though David's and my backgrounds were similar, our personalities were different.

He was more laid back than I. I was quick tempered and always into something—it was our environments that made us similar. His folks in Birmingham thought it would be better for him to leave Birmingham and move to Tuscaloosa, so I decided I would leave straight from Georgia and move to Tuscaloosa, as well.

We had about a three-week spread before we had to report for fall practice. Summer school was still in session, and a few of the players were on campus so David and I met up in Tuscaloosa. After my last trip to Prichard when my case was dismissed, I knew I wasn't going to stay in Prichard. I grabbed ten thousand of the twenty-five, and returned to Georgia, gave my sister her money, and headed to Tuscaloosa with the rest. By the time I arrived, David had already been there a few days, so he was able to show me around as I drove. He was already working a little job at a grocery store and living with two young white guys in an apartment off campus—they attended 'Bama, too. The first night we stayed there after hanging out with a few of the players, I went to my first college-style party—an end-of-summer gig. It was a mixed crowd—white, blacks, and others, and we visited fraternities and sororities, moving from house to house, meeting people. In one of those houses, I met a young lady whom I thought was quite attractive—she was short, light-skinned, and from Montgomery, Alabama. Two years older than I, she was going into her junior year of college, and she gave me her number—I called her the following day.

Chapter 11
College Experience

When visiting Division 1 Schools as a highly recruited athlete, it's different than going as an academic scholar. As athletes, campus tour guides didn't show us the campus library or book store—or, classrooms. So, when I arrived from a small high school in Prichard to attend the Division 1 University of Alabama, it was a bit of a culture shock. An official visit provided only a snippet real college life and, like most freshman, I expected a sense of freedom—no curfew, no one telling me what to do, and getting up when I felt like it. I viewed college as a right of passage, and I was ready to make the most of it.

My first year at 'Bama started well. I already had a few parties under my belt, and I looked forward to competing for playing time on the football team. When I went in as a freshman, I was the fifth running back on the depth chart, and three out of the four running backs before me went on to play in the NFL. It was clear I had my work cut out for me, but I refused to be red shirted—it would be embarrassing, and it wouldn't show the coach I had what it took to be a valuable member of the team.

Our running back coach was typical—he used seniority to justify his reasons for the order of the depth chart. As a freshman, I wanted to get on the field and play—besides, I signed with 'Bama to play, not to wait until my second year.

Football was my number one priority, but it seemed no matter where I lived the street was always a part of my life. That, and partying—the summertime partying carried over into the season although I viewed it differently from my high school years. I didn't party, hustle, or do much of anything during football season—with Birmingham only a forty-five minute drive from school, it was easy to meet people similar to the guys from my old neighborhood.

I had connections.

David and I made several trips to Birmingham to hang out with his family, or guys who were into hustling dope— much like the guys who supported me when I was in high school. It was obvious David's and my backgrounds were similar—so similar that each time we visited Birmingham, we stopped to chat with guys who were hustling. I admit it wasn't the best environment—despite my commitment to football, we drank a lot of beer, smoked a lot of weed, and I gave little thought to how I should live my life.

When the season started, the same guys attended the games and our families met beforehand so they could sit together. David's mom and my mom became good friends, and Mom always appreciated his mom's taking me in as if I were one of her own. Ever since I left Georgia, they were the only family I had on that end, and I couldn't return to Prichard and run the risk of getting into some sort of trouble. Plus, I really didn't want to go back to Prichard. I found something new and better—for once, I didn't miss the wars and hustling on the block, but there were certain things about Prichard I did miss. I missed my son, spending time with him, and his mother. We were still a couple at the beginning of my college days, and I tried to call to check on them every day. Because Prichard was a hotbed of trouble for me, Mom brought them to see me whenever she could. In fact, she did just about anything to keep me from going back to Prichard.

Even though I was at college, I still had responsibilities in Mobile. My girl who was pregnant didn't get the attention I gave my son's mother because no one knew she existed. The main reason we didn't have a relationship was the lifestyle I was trying to put behind me and, after leaving for college, our communication dwindled significantly. I felt terrible because I couldn't be there for her like I was for my first child and his mother.

It was a tough spot for a seventeen year old.

Truth was I had to make some tough decisions, as well as weigh my options. I knew there was no way I could focus on that situation and be a student, football player, and the father of two children with two different girls. Fortunately, the mother of my second child had a good support system with her mother, father, sister, and three brothers living in the house. I was grateful they were there to take up the slack for there was no way I could be in Mobile, and play football for Alabama at the same time. So, I decided to disconnect the relationship with my second child's mother—I didn't know what else to do. I figured I could make up for lost time once I made it through college, and settled into life. I decided I would put more energy in the relationship with my son's mother, but I still had to figure out how I was going to be a part of their lives while living in two different cities.

I never owned a bank account—in the hood, we always

dealt in cash, and used a stash spot for our deposits and withdrawals. Banks? Only if you were a fool. Later, I learned that manner of thinking was ingrained in us because of the pervasive ignorance of poverty-stricken environments. I didn't consider opening a bank account until one day when David and I were hanging out with two white guys. One of them noticed I carried a large sum of cash money, and he asked me questions about it—*why was I carrying so much cash? Why not put it in the bank?* When I told him, he laughed and explained the real purposes of the banks. Checks. Debit cards. Interest. I'm sure my mother had a bank account and checks, but she didn't share financial information, so the subject never came up. When the white guy explained how everything worked, it all made sense. He told me about a program the banks offered to college students—I could open an account with only $100, and I would receive unlimited checks and a debit card. The only negative thing was I was only seventeen, and I couldn't sign for it until I was eighteen—luckily, my birthday was only a couple of weeks away.

I went for it, and decided to give it a try—I figured if they stole $100 from me, I could live with it. So, on my eighteenth birthday I opened my first bank account using my mother's address. When the checks and debit card arrived, she delivered them when she came to visit— it was then I decided that was how I was going to send money home to my son's mother. She had a job working at McDonald's, so she was familiar with cashing checks. Our new system worked well and, after a few checks, I decided to put $5000 of the $7000 I had with me in the bank. I couldn't bring myself to put everything in the bank in case the old poverty ignorance thing were true.

Even though I had money, I didn't have to spend much when I was with David because the guys we hung out with from his neighborhood were big dope boys—they bought us whatever we wanted, and lined our pockets with money. I was tempted on several occasions to ask one of them to let me cop some product and flip $5000, but I never liked to hustle during football season. Plus, I was in a foreign land and didn't have a spot to operate. But, the main thing? I needed to kill that lifestyle. One of the main reasons I stayed away from Mobile was staring me in the face in Birmingham.

I stayed strong and continued to focus on football, keeping my grades up so I could stay on the field. When the first week of August rolled around, incoming freshman were to report for fall practice. When the rest of our classmates arrived, David and I acted as tour guides since we had already been there a few weeks. The football and basketball players lived in the athletic dorms—upperclassmen lived on the first and second floors, and freshman and basketball players lived on the third, or top floor. Our freshman class was the strongest class ever playing at 'Bama because we had seventeen of our twenty-five players who were true freshman—that made us a tightly knit group.

College was a different gig—even though the University of Alabama enforced hard and fast rules, I didn't have any trouble breaking them. Then, I didn't think about my behavior not being in the best interests of the university—now I know I entered college with the wrong mindset and, if I had it all to do over again, I would respect the great institution of the University of Alabama. And, that goes for the coaches, too—I never considered breaking the rules was disrespectful to our head coach, or to the other coaches on the team. The truth is the university and coaches were completely unaware of how I broke their rules—and, I'm certain if they had an inkling of what I did, I would have had a one-way ticket out.

We made ourselves known as soon as we hit the dorm. Upperclassmen told us we were wilder than other freshman classes, and we did things never done before. We stashed cases of beer in our room because it was the hang out spot—David and I were roommates and, many nights, he headed to Birmingham after practice to be with his kids and their momma—that meant I had the room to myself, and I was ready to party. By the time the upperclassmen reported a few days later, we had already set the tone for the year.

The upperclassmen talked about initiation and hazing the freshmen—a many-year tradition—but our class wasn't having any of it. It was hard to catch us alone and, if they came at one of us, they had to deal with all of us! David and I were the leaders, so we were their main targets. It were as if we lived in our own world—a third world—so we called our class the Third World Posse, and the rest of the team knew us as such. We took it seriously, and defended the Third World Posse as if our lives depended on it!

Our team was good that year, and I played as a true freshman. I was successful on the field, but it was a tough go in the classroom, and I soon discovered effective time management was an issue for me. I never had a problem keeping up with classes while in high school simply because the work was easier, and I didn't party as much. My math grades on the college entrance exam forced me into a remedial math class, and that was okay—except I hated it was at eight o'clock in the morning, and the credit hours didn't count toward graduation. Good thing was it counted toward my overall GPA because for players on scholarship, maintaining a 2.0 grade point average was mandatory.

The work was easy, but arriving at class at eight o'clock wasn't, and if I missed a certain number of days

I automatically failed the class. There was one good motivation, though—a girl from Birmingham who was in the class with me. A pretty girl, we became friends, started dating, and often studied together. The one thing I learned from the entire experience was that I would never again schedule a class for eight o'clock in the morning—no way!

That season we finished 11-1—our only loss was to Steve Spurrier and the Florida Gators, and it was a game we should have won. The success of our year earned us a bowl bid to play in the Blockbuster Bowl sponsored by Blockbuster Video Entertainment. We played the game in Joe Robbie Stadium in Miami, Florida, and I was somewhat familiar with Miami since I traveled there a couple of times while I was in high school to pick up some cocaine. But, I was never there to hang out and kick it. I no longer had any contacts, plus I was a college student living a new life separate from drugs and crime.

I made a concerted effort to live the square life and, to be honest, I enjoyed it better—more peace, less stress. We played the Colorado Buffaloes in the Blockbuster Bowl, taking the victory and finishing the season 12-1. Yes, I had a good year, but nothing great happened—I scored two touchdowns, and ran 100 yards playing on special teams with limited playing time. But, I wasn't discouraged because since the starting running back graduated, I figured the starting job would be up for grabs the following season.

As I eased into my sophomore year, the depth chart changed. One guy transferred to a different school, so that left the three of us from the previous season and we were listed according to seniority. The guy who was #1 on the chart was pretty good, but I always thought I was a better running back than the #2 guy. I was the third back.

The entire year I never went back to Mobile, but I did

stay in touch with the streets. Through the grapevine, I learned the Feds swooped through and scooped up all the dealers on secret indictments. They were getting long sentences for dealing crack because at that time crack was a one hundred to one ratio to cocaine. I talked to one of my childhood friends, and he said the Feds were doling out thirty-year-to-life sentences. He also told me if I ever decided to hustle again, I shouldn't sell crack simply based on a ridiculous possible prison sentence—cocaine and weed were safer. Of course, until I told him, he had no way of knowing I was finished with the game, and I was trying to make it to the NFL. I didn't want to hustle again! To prove it to myself, after my freshman season I stopped drinking and smoking weed, and I realized it was the best way to get out of the game and never return. I decided to totally dedicate myself to football—school was important, but it was secondary to football.

The NFL was my only chance.

By the summer after my freshman year, I still hadn't returned to Prichard. That year, I stayed in school for summer session, and began dating a girl from Chicago. Even though I had a dorm room, I stayed with her most nights, and we had a good relationship. I swear, she was the prettiest girl I ever met—sweet and kind, I wondered how I managed to get so lucky! She and I often hit the town, and I learned how to get around the city more, in addition to meeting local folks in Tuscaloosa. Local rappers, too—we got haircuts at the same barbershop.

That spring, many of the former players who made it to the NFL returned for the Spring A-Day game and picnic—a 'Bama tradition I hoped to continue. Hearing their stories about the NFL was great motivation as I dove into my sophomore season and, as I immersed myself into the rigors of football practice and games, I reaffirmed my vow to lay off drinking or smoking until we won the National Championship title. I won a State Championship in high school, and I thought because of the way our team was built we could achieve the title that year. The process reminded me my high school team which was one of the main reasons I signed with 'Bama—we had the team to make it happen.

The preseason ranked 'Bama number 23 in the AP Poll, and the Third World Posse had a full year's experience. I was third on the depth chart and, when the season started, I hoped to be #1 or #2. The guy holding the #1 spot was a legitimate running back but, in the past, had a problem staying healthy. The #2 player was decent, but I felt I was better. It didn't help he was one of Coach's favorites—he was the coach's pet as well as a year ahead of me in class. Unfortunately, our coach believed in the seniority stuff.

Heading into the season I stopped much of the partying I did as a freshman, but I was still dating the girl from Chicago. My oldest child's mother and I decided a long distance relationship wasn't going to work for us, although I still had a responsibility to take care of my child. After much discussion, we agreed my major responsibility was to pay for his day care, and I was glad to do so.

One of the things interesting about college was while attending 'Bama on a full scholarship, I couldn't get a job, and I decided I no longer wanted to hustle in the streets. Even though a full scholarship covered everything dealing with school expenses, it didn't leave room for outside expenses—it didn't cover laundry, dinner and a movie, nor any other miscellaneous thing a young man in college would like to do. Since I was young, I always managed my money well and I still had the money I hustled the previous year. Plus, I added to it from other people who gave me a few dollars here and there. I realized I had to I budget my money so I could cover my son's day care without feeling the pressures of having to get back out in the street to hustle. I really wanted that chapter of my life to be over.

Finally, the season started—expectations were high because we were coming off a season with only one loss. The only thing to better a one-loss season was finishing undefeated, thereby winning the National Title. The team we lost to the year before wasn't on our season schedule, and we thought we could beat every other team. However, we weren't ranked in the top ten, and we barely made the top 25—even so, we started the season on a roll winning by three in a row. The first three games I scored three touchdowns, and I had good playing time since I was third on the depth chart and, even though I was third, I was first for touchdowns. A few of our games were low scoring because our offense wasn't explosive, but our defense was first all across the board. Not to mention we had the best field goal kickers in the nation.

One day while David and I were sitting in our room, we decided to come up with an endzone celebration—up until then, we were the only two who crossed into the endzone. An endzone celebration seemed the natural thing to do—too bad neither one of us scored a touchdown during the next game! So, our idea was on hold for at least another week. Finally, I scored my fourth touchdown when we were on the road to New Orleans playing against the Tulane Green Wave. That was when I unveiled what became a household phrase—the *Sherman Shake.*

My signature.

I did endzone celebrations in high school, but on the college stage I received Division One national exposure and I instantly became the fans' favorite. After that, no matter where we played, fans approached me asking me to do the Sherman Shake. All ages, too! Little boys to sixty-year-old ladies! It was fun, but I wondered if it were the only thing our fans looked forward to because our offense was so boring. Our QB was a first year full-time starter, and the coaches didn't trust him to throw the ball. We were eighty percent run oriented which is why being third on the chart wasn't that bad—there were plenty of carries to spread around.

As the season progressed my performance increased and, although I was #3, my stats were better than #2. Even so, Coach wouldn't change the rotation, but it didn't matter to me as long as I had the time needed to get it done. We inched up in the ranking, beating good teams ranked ahead of us. One team was the Tennessee Volunteers, ranked in the top ten when we beat them, and that win placed us inside the top ten in 1992, as well. We went on to finish the regular season undefeated, and that year was also the first year of the SEC Championship game. The SEC was divided into an East and West, six and six—we won the West, and Florida won the East—the one team we lost to the year before. It was a classic match-up—Steve Spurrier led the #1 offense, and Gene Stallings led the #1 defense. By the time of the game, we ranked #3 and we needed to win the game to qualify to play for the national title. If we lost, we not only lost the opportunity, but also the SEC Championship. Before the 1992 season, an undefeated record throughout the regular season automatically catapulted us to SEC Champions.

Once again, it was the story of our season—we went on to win the game on a defensive touchdown. At the time, the Miami Hurricanes was the #1 team in the nation with a Heisman trophy-winning QB. After the Florida win, we ranked #2 in the polls.

The game was set as #1 vs. #2, and 'Bama entered the game as a huge underdog. Most of the country didn't give us a fighting chance against those guys—they owned the high powered explosive offense, and all we had was the #1 defense in the nation as well as an offensive run machine. David and I had a pretty good game—he had a good kick return to set me up for the first touchdown of the game, and that's when the Sherman Shake became a household thing. Our defense did a fantastic job, and some of the best defensive plays in school history took place during that game. We ended up overcoming the odds with a 34-13 victory to become the 1992 College Football National Champs! I finished the season well, second on the team for touchdowns, and I became a person of interest with the Sherman Shake.

The preceding year, I affirmed I wouldn't drink or smoke until after we won the national title—the night after the game, I went out to celebrate! I had a few drinks and, after not drinking alcohol for a year, it was easy to feel the buzz. We popped champagne and smoked cigars, and my godbrother hung out with us that night. He went to Miami to be a civil defense lawyer, and after law school he decided to live there. He attended the game and thought Miami would beat us—turned out he was responsible for paying for our drinks that night!

The celebration parties continued for a couple of weeks, and when students returned from Christmas break, there was nothing but parties! The bad thing was I fell back into the party scene—I set my classes so I didn't have to get up until ten o'clock on Mondays, Wednesdays, and Fridays, and after noon on Tuesdays and Thursdays. It didn't take long for me to regress to my partying ways, and it wasn't long before I drank and smoked as much as I did before my year's sabbatical. The saying is true—*old habits die hard*. We partied hard all the way up until spring practice and, as a result, a few members of the Third World Posse were placed on academic probation and removed from the dorm.

Once spring practice started, I put things back in the proper prospective—I didn't stop completely, but I did slow down. But, before I began my football regimen, I met a few local folks from Tuscaloosa—a group of young women that supplied the city with good marijuana from Texas. After practice, I went to their houses, sat with their families, and their parents always treated me as if I were one of their own. I spent a lot of time with these chicks, and when I started dating one of them, I found myself spending more time off campus than on campus—so much time, in fact, I started to feel like a local. My girlfriend's mother loved me to death, always wanting me to come over so she could cook me something to eat. I often spent the night at their house, and became one of the family. Did their families know what these girls did for money? I don't know. All I know is that group of girls had a good grip on the marijuana surging into the city and, without knowing my past, they looked at me as a football player and college student. That was it, and I preferred it stay that way. Between my desire for not wanting to return to Prichard and wanting to be with my girlfriend's family, I always stayed in school during the summer. It worked out well because I had my local family, and I still budgeted money—by attending summer school I received money from school funds, and every little bit helped.

Spring practice came and went, and when the fall season returned I was still #2 on the depth chart. That didn't bother me because I knew I would get the ball just as many times, or more. In my mind and soul I knew I was a better running back than the guy who was ahead of me on the chart. Everyone else knew it as well, but with their being stuck on seniority, the depth chart didn't change until the fourth game of the season when the obvious became visual. For the first three games, I racked up over 100 yards in each game and, over the three games, he may have had a combined 100 yards. He was a senior, and I know the coach wanted him to play, but the good thing was the head coach wanted to win—he believed in playing the best players and, in the third game, the stats didn't lie. As luck would have it, my competition suffered an ankle injury and couldn't play the fourth game. I became the starter, and my goal that year was to rush for one thousand yards in the SEC. When a back rushed a thousand yards in the SEC, going pro was almost a done deal. The SEC was the toughest conference in college football for many years—we were coming off a national title, and we still weren't ranked #1. Being defending champs made us a target for other schools to play their best, so every week was a tough game for our team.

The third week in October threatened our twenty-plus game winning streak. It was tradition for us to play Tennessee, and we ended up with a draw against them. By then, we lost our starting QB for the season, so David had to step in to play quarterback. He made a last minute play to tie the game, and it turned out to be my worst game to date that season—I rushed for fifty nine yards that game, and if I rushed for one hundred yards or more in a game, there was a ninety percent chance we would win. Not even close.

Our first loss actually came a few weeks later against LSU when I suffered an injury in the first quarter of the game, forcing me to miss the next two games, one of which was the Iron Bowl against Auburn. It was the first time I lost to Auburn in my college career, and our overall record ended up being 8-2-1. Not what we hoped, but we were still bowl eligible. We accepted the bowl bid to play in the Gator Bowl in Jacksonville, Florida and, by then, I was back playing at my normal speed. We beat the North Carolina Tar Heels, I rushed for one hundred plus yards, and scored a couple touchdowns calling for the celebratory Sherman Shake. Nonetheless, I failed to make my goal of one thousand yards. At one point in the season, I thought I might turn pro at the end, but, with the injury, it was best I stayed. Sadly, David left us behind, and by the end of season I wasn't sure if I would ever go pro.

My partying, drinking, and smoking carried over into the offseason, and I hung out with the local crew as well the click of chicks that was moving weed in the city. We hung out almost everyday drinking and smoking weed but, luckily, I was still in a relationship, and she wound up helping me quite a bit. I wasn't focused, and she helped me complete all of my class work. Truth is I don't know if I could have completed everything if it weren't for her. I signed up to run track for the school during the offseason, but I ran the 60 meter for the indoor season only because outdoor season interfered with football spring practice.

That year, I was in the mood to try things—as the offseason progressed, I got better acquainted with the local chicks. I was familiar with the drug trade, but not the marijuana trade—they explained it, and asked if it were something that interested me. Previously, I hustled on the block with crack cocaine—different from hustling pot—but I didn't know the weed market. Being on scholarship we couldn't get jobs or sell our autographs, nor could we accept gifts from anyone. Bottom line was I didn't have any money coming in from anywhere. During the season, I purchased a Jeep Cherokee and was spending money playing cards.

My budgeting skills? Nosedived.

It was probably a given I wanted to invest into the weed game—a few pounds, flip the money. I started out by buying three to four pounds, and worked my way up to ten. Back then, ten pounds sold for $4500—I gave the ladies $1000 to hustle it for me, and kept $2000 for myself.

We did this at least twice a month.

Between the time I left Prichard and hit Tuscaloosa, I seldom went back to my hometown. After my homeboys telling me not to get caught up in crack because of the possible prison time, I knew I wouldn't sell crack again in my life. But, the way the weed was moving, I thought if football didn't take me where I needed to be, then hustling weed would be my ticket. To be honest, the NFL seemed so far fetched—it was a hit and miss league without guarantees, and it made sense to keep hustling as an option. I thought if I didn't make the NFL, I could graduate and become a coach, or a health education teacher.

The spring of '94 was busy for me—running track, hustling marijuana, spring football practice, and going to classes in an effort to make good grades. Coming out of spring practice I made it to #1 on the depth chart, and I wasn't there only because of seniority—I was the best we had because none of the boys behind me made it to the NFL.

During this time, the hustling game was good—within three months, I hustled marijuana to the tune of ten to fifteen grand. My girlfriend managed to keep me eligible so I didn't need to attend any summer classes, and I decided to move to Miami so I could concentrate on working out as well as getting ready for my senior season. My godbrother helped me find good trainers and I was also running track on a summer track team, so I did everything to become stronger and more fit.

I trained twice a day, Monday through Friday. The trainers worked me hard, and I was in the best shape of my life. There was no denying I was at my best playing weight while I was in Miami, and I pinpointed my focus on getting in the best shape possible.

I was looking forward to my senior season.

Chapter 12
Winding Down College

One of the best things about winning the National Championship was the chance to visit with the President of the United States. When we won the National Title, William Jefferson Clinton was the president, and I thought he was cool. He was my favorite president then, and he's still my favorite now. In 1992 I could vote for the first time, and Clinton was my pick. He won the election, and it was great to have dinner on the White House lawn with the president—plus, it was my first visit to Washington D.C. Granted, I was young, but it was one of the most exciting experiences in my life. We took the grand tour of the White House, privy to things we will never see on television. I also met all the cabinet members, senators, and congressmen. Talk about great motivators to reach the National Championship!

My senior year was coming off the worst year since I enrolled at Alabama. We played the SEC Championship game and lost to the Florida Gators, and went on to finish the season 10-2-1. Losing two games in the same year was unacceptable at Alabama because expectations were high from fans and coaches, as well as my fellow team members. Going into the 1994 season, we were a team full of no namers. However, we had a great nucleus—Third World Posse members were seniors, and the quarterback and fullback from the class of 1990 were back for their red shirt senior season. Plus, we had a couple of freshmen making a solid contribution. Even though we were rough around the edges, I felt as if we had a good chance to win as much as any other team in the country.

It was my first season as the clear number one guy in the backfield, and I was working for a new running back coach. The field was wide open, and if I weren't the best back he had he wouldn't have put me in the top position. He displayed zero favoritism which was interesting because when he joined our coaching staff, he was already aware of me. We had the same last name, so we considered our being related in some way, but we weren't. Bottom line was he was a good coach, and I respected him.

That year, I was in the best shape of my life. I committed to being the best football player I could, and I trained in Miami for the summer—plus, I didn't drink, smoke, or hustle on the block. Quite a few kids stayed in the city for summer school and, since they were there, they decided to organize a back to school block party in the lot of the student center—The Furg. It turned out to be an interesting evening, and I had no idea the two women I met would become important people in my life! One was from Montgomery, the other from Birmingham, and both were sweet young ladies.

On that particular night everyone was out to have a good time, so it was a huge party with lots of drinking and smoking. It so happened I was traveling with a couple of guys on the team at the time—I owned a Caddy and a pearl white Jeep Cherokee complete with AMG spoiler and deep dish hammer wheels—and, I decided to drive my Jeep that night. The guys I was with were drinking gin and juice, and it was obvious the two girls were drinking, possibly the same thing. It was funny—the guys drank most of their liquor, but they didn't have enough juice, and the girls experienced just the opposite. They had plenty of juice, but not enough booze! With the season right around the corner, I was still in discipline mode regarding drinking and smoking, so my friend thought it would be a good idea for me to ask the girls if they had more gin. "If I had some juice," one girl replied, so we traded—and that was the beginning of some life-long relationships!

Entering my senior year was a different from all other years because David wasn't with me, and it was weird not having him there to listen to and comment on my ideas. After he left, I decided I wouldn't have another roommate, so I talked to Coach about it and he understood. I was allowed to have the room David and I shared to myself, and the good thing about it was most of the Third World Posse was still around. A couple of them transferred, and one or two lost their scholarships due poor academic performance. Nonetheless, as a whole, we were still holding it down and I still had a group I trusted.

When we reported to practice each year after summer break, we had to pass a conditioning test and, going into my senior season, I felt good about our chances to win. Players always sweated the conditioning test and, normally, I would be concerned. The test usually consisted of running within a specific period of time—for example, one year we had to complete eight 200 yard sprints in 34 seconds with a 45 second rest time in between each sprint. It was tough, but the test going into my senior year was supposed to be tougher. It was. Luckily, I was in such great physical condition I ran the test with my teammates as a warm up to my workout. The strength and conditioning coaches were impressed at the ease with which I completed the test, especially when other players struggled to pass. The rub was if we didn't pass the test the first time, we had to run it again—that alone served as a great motivation to get through it the first time around!

My time spent training in Miami was worth it, and I continued to do everything I could to make it to the NFL. My mindset was one of participating in boot camp— military boot camp is twelve weeks, the season was twelve games. Make it through that, and I would graduate to the NFL. As a day-dreaming kid from Prichard, it was good to know my dream of becoming an NFL player may soon be a reality. I knew if I did everything I was supposed to do, I would make it—and if, for some reason, I didn't make it, I wouldn't have any regrets because I gave it my best.

Playing in the SEC for the University of Alabama had its advantages, one of which was having a program that produced quite a few NFL players. Scouts and sports agents always came around us, and we had to be careful not to accept gifts or money. I'll say this—as a student with zero income and all expenses paid via scholarship, it was hard to resist when someone contacted me armed with fists full of bucks. Truth is, I didn't resist, but during my senior season I didn't want to take any chances on being suspended for the season or a game. Plus, I had a cushion of money in the bank—enough to carry me through the season. I saved over $50,000 in my account from when I hustled with the local group of ladies.

Another thing that made me feel secure about the season was the insurance policy I had—the university couldn't insure me, but I could take out a policy on myself. In fact, my coach couldn't even go with me to the bank—I had to meet with the bankers, and arrange to borrow the money—then I pledged the bonus money I received from being drafted within the first three rounds. The NCAA passed a rule saying a senior projected to be in the top three rounds could borrow money from a bank, and pledge that money to his bonus money. That way, I was protected against a career-ending injury. The NCAA has strict rules regarding insurance and, for once in my life, I figured it was in my best interest to follow them.

By the time the season started, the media made their expectations known. We went into the 1994 season ranked just outside the top ten at #11. Unranked Tennessee Chattanooga was our opener, posing no match for the experience of our team.   During that time we were still playing some of our home games at Legion Field in Birmingham, Alabama, and it was typical for a powerhouse school to start the season off with a lesser opponent. Doing so gave the more inexperienced players field time before meeting the tougher conference teams.

The opening game was the first time I was the #1 featured running back—the job was all mine, and I earned it! I worked hard during the off season to be in that position and, in my mind, it was the beginning of an opportunity to show everyone what I could really do. Although the game wasn't televised nationally, stadium attendance that day was over 82,000, and the local stations made sure to cover it, ensuring a wide-spread audience.

The first five minutes of the game was good—the rest of it, not so much. The separation of talent was apparent, and by the time the fourth quarter rolled around, the game was out of hand. I rushed for over 150 yards, coupled with a pair of touchdowns, and the final score ended up being 42-14. One of the girls I met at the back to school block party was at the game, and I made eye contact with her acknowledging her with a slight nod. She responded with a smile and a wave. Naturally, I thought about calling her when I returned to campus!

When a game gets so out of hand, it's customary for the winning team to call off the dogs and use reserves to close out the game. In fact, Coach Stallings was notorious for doing just that—securing a lead and sitting on it. Everyone knew it, including the Vegas odd makers— that's why they wouldn't give us a large point spread.

As much as we enjoyed the easy win, the tide turned (pardon the pun!) during our second game. We were still the home team, but that week we played in Tuscaloosa on natural grass at Bryant-Denny Stadium. Artificial turf fields were nice, but the grass field always felt better to me—turf was fast, but with speed came a much higher chance for injury. More than once I saw players carted off with torn knee ligaments all because of the turf field. So, natural grass was a welcomed change!

Our second opponent, Vanderbilt, was a team from our own conference, and we learned when we played an SEC team we never took them for granted. Vanderbilt was solid, albeit a less talented team in the conference. Nevertheless, we had to prepare to expect our opponents' best efforts. We entered the game still ranked at #11, not having cracked the top 10 because, until then, we only played one game against an unranked team. Vanderbilt was a school more known for academics—not football. They seemed more smart than talented, however it turned into a hard fought game. I rushed for over 120 yards and scored a touchdown—but, we had to keep the starters in until the end of the game. We ended up kicking a late field goal to make the final score a ten point lead, 17-7, taking home the win. If that game were a year earlier, I would have wowed the crowd with the Sherman Shake three times—but, during the off season, the NCAA instituted a rule stating any player performing an endzone celebration would cost their team a fifteen-yard penalty to be accessed on the kick off. As much as I enjoyed celebrating after every touchdown, it wasn't worth piling a penalty onto the team, especially if it cost our team the game. Not only that, I was determined to end the season as National Champions. So, we won the game, and everyone was excited about our chance to return to the top.

Our team was a tightly-knit group of players, and we'd coordinate with each other about where to hang out afterward. We went our separate ways, meeting with family who attended the game, reconnecting later at the Citizens Club. When I arrived at the club, I ran into my circle of local girls—nice, since I didn't have a chance to hang with them since my return from Miami. There really wasn't a reason to since I wasn't hustling, but, I admit, it was good to hang out with them. Eighty percent of my focus was on making it to the NFL, and the other twenty percent was on having a good time. That particular evening, I became a casual weed smoker—until then I neither drank nor smoked since before the summer. Can you blame me? I was feeling good about the win and wanted to celebrate a little. The girls were still hustling weed, and they always asked me if I still wanted a piece of the action. I was focused on trying to do all I could to make it to the NFL, but, with that being an uncertainty, I was tempted on a few occasions. Hustling was easy money, and since the last time I was in the game with them the profit increased exponentially. The girls had strong clients, and even though I wasn't actually participating, I wanted to stay close to the hustle just in case football didn't work out. Crack? Never. Weed? Maybe. I knew I would never sell crack another day on my life. That night I picked back up on a weed smoking habit, and the girls and I started hanging out more. All the while, however, I never lost my focus on football.

I would lay my life on the line for it.

I was having a good season to this point. We were 2-0 as a team, and I ran for over 100 yards in both games. Our third game was also a conference game, but it was our first road game of the season—a hostile environment. Our game against Vanderbilt was so close that we dropped a spot from #11 to #12 in the country. However, Arkansas wasn't a ranked team, but they felt if they could beat us their whole season would be complete. In fact, most teams we played felt that way. We were ready, though—the Razorbacks brought their game, and we escaped with a six point win after I rushed for over 150 yards, 100 yards receiving, and scored my longest play from scrimmage when I took a pass seventy-three yards for a touchdown. The final score was 13-6.

When we got back to the bus and rode to the airport, Coach told us the owner of the Dallas Cowboys, Jerry Jones, was at the game. When we arrived at the airport, we looked out the window and saw Jerry's personal plane painted like a Dallas Cowboy uniform. I was thrilled to see it because I was a Cowboy fan all of my life, and I dreamed of being picked by them in the draft. Seeing his plane reaffirmed belief in myself that I could do it, and nothing was going to stand in my way!

When the rankings came out after the game, we regained the #11 spot. But, I felt we could do better. The following week, we returned to Birmingham to play another unranked team, the Tulane Greenwave, and I achieved a personal best of 193 yards, and two touchdowns. We walked with a 20-10 victory, heading into one of the best games we played that season. It was back to Bryan-Denny Stadium for the first night game—6:30 prime time on ESPN against the Georgia Bulldogs, a talented team.

We knew it was going to be a dog fight, and we were right. Georgia wasn't ranked in the top 25 when we met, but they had a couple of players on their team who would go on to have productive years playing in the NFL.

Turned out the Georgia game was our toughest competitor thus far, even though they weren't a ranked SEC team. Whenever two powerhouse programs in the conference meet there is always a potential upset, and the rules of separation are thin. Maybe a bonehead play. Maybe the coach was a tad bit better. Maybe a key player was out due to injury. Whatever the case, there was no exception to the game we played against Georgia in 1994. The Bulldogs featured one of the best quarterbacks in the country as well as a defense that could play against any team in the nation.

We knew ESPN didn't pick up games fans wouldn't be interested in, but 'Bama was a senior-led team with solid, true freshman to contribute. We pulled off some hard-fought games with lesser talented teams such as Arkansas and Tulane and, with that game being played on campus in the city of Tuscaloosa, there were a few added distractions such as trying to make sure everyone from home attending the game got tickets, plus the after-game functions. If we lost the game, the atmosphere wouldn't be as festive—but, my, oh my! If we won, the parties would be cranking! I still wasn't drinking alcohol, and since my mother and sisters would be in town for the game, as well as my godbrother from Miami, I knew I would have to spend time with them.

During this time I was still seeing my girlfriend from Huntsville, but things between us weren't good. For some reason, she couldn't understand why I didn't give her the attention I had before I left for the summer to go to train in Miami. I tried to explain my focus had to be on football if I wanted to make it to the next level. Football, at that time, was first above everything—except God. Even my education took a back seat to football. I always felt I chose to attend the University of Alabama because I would have the best chance to win—and, winning would give me the exposure I needed to further my career. If I wanted to concentrate on education and play in the SEC, I would have attended Vanderbilt to be an engineer—or, something. I made up in my mind that before I allowed a relationship with a girl to distract me, I would rather separate from the relationship. Well, that was easier said than done because I developed serious feelings for her, and it was difficult for me to walk away. Not only that, my family was attached to her and that made things worse. She and my sister were friends, visiting and planning trips without me. I confess, it got under my skin—not because they were good friends, but because my sister always had the habit of ratting me out. Every time my girlfriend came back from visiting with my sister, she complained about something. I tired of it, and I recognized I had to extricate myself from the relationship. I certainly couldn't dump my sister, but girlfriends could be replaced—about that time, I started to look for a replacement.

It didn't make sense to invest much time into looking for that girl because I was in full focus on football. Yes, there were two potential candidates with whom I became friends earlier that year when I went to the back to school block party. Both were attractive and smart, and they were to graduate a year later than I. But, until my previous girlfriend and I parted, I didn't speak to either of them since the block party. From my occasional weed smoking, I reconnected with the local girl with whom I hustled the weed throughout the previous years. She and I had always had a good understanding about where we stood with each other, and we had fun hanging out, making money, and we were good friends. Her family was like my family, and her mother always treated me like one of and her own. And, her siblings treated me like a brother on those lonely holidays when the campus was empty. They always welcomed me to join their family for Christmas or Thanksgiving dinner and, if I needed a place to sleep, I was always welcome then, too. It was like that from the beginning, and it were as if I were adopted—to this day, I appreciate their kindness. Our families were so similar, it wasn't a difficult stretch to think of them as my extended family. They always preferred to watch my games from home, inviting me to stop by after the games.

I did.

Outside of the normal home game distractions, we prepared for the Georgia game the same as all the rest of the games. But, the way the game started out it seemed as if we didn't prepare at all! The opening drive Georgia got the ball, driving the length of the field to score a touchdown. We scored. Tie. But the next series gave Georgia the ball, and they took advantage of it, going up by 14-7 lead. Our turn. Three up. Three down. It was a slap in the face that motivated our defense, but the next time Georgia got the ball they ended the drive with a 21-7 lead. Just before the half, we scored a field goal to make the score 21-10. I carried the ball over ten times for ten yards—one yard a carry. Acceptable, but not great.

Being down double digits at halftime wasn't a good feeling. So, we adjusted our game and our offense came

alive. We shifted the momentum, going on to shock the
Bulldogs with another victory. We walked away with a
last minute field goal—29-28. Everyone was ecstatic! The
city was alive, and I was ready to celebrate even though
statistically it was one of my worst games. I finished with
over 100 all-purpose yards, but only 30 yards rushing and
no touchdowns. My goal for that year was to rush for over
100 yards in every game. Unfortunately, Georgia squirreled
that idea when they realized from watching our game films
that containing me would give them a good chance to win.
Little did they know our quarterback was going to have
such a good game—they chose to stack the box and rely on
one-on-one coverage in the secondary, allowing us to come
from two touchdowns down to win the game.

After a come-from-behind victory, the city was filled
with joy, and after-game activities were slated to be more
fun than usual! Even though I was disappointed in my
performance, I was happy we won the game and the hope
of winning another national title was still alive. I located
my mom and the rest of the family, and rode to the hotel
with them to hang out. Mom was always intense about my
games, and she let me know what happened while I was
involved with other aspects of the game.

After making sure she was settled in, I swung by my
other mom's house where I hooked up with my local female
friend. Because of the rigors of the football season, we didn't
spend much time together, and I didn't go to her house
much, either—which was a little strange because when we
were hustling together the year before, we decided to pitch
in and purchase a little spot where we could hang out and
chill, and I hadn't been there since I was back in T-town.
So, it seemed a celebration there was a great idea! I told
a couple guys from the team, and she called some of her
girlfriends—my godbrother was there, too, and all of us

hung out and smoked weed all night long. We partied hard because everyone who was celebrating our game knew the next day would be all business—time to prepare for the next game.

Our next game was to be played in Tuscaloosa's Bryant-Denny Stadium, and it was going to be 'goin' on' just like the week prior. We faced a non-conference opponent in Southern Mississippi, and I hoped to get back on track by gaining over 100 yards. Southern Miss was always known for playing us tough, and we couldn't rest on our laurels because of our previous victories. It wasn't a time to take anything for granted and, as it turned out, the game was everything people said it would be.

With the game being earlier in the day, it gave us more time to spend with our families who came to town to visit. Unlike the Georgia game, we anticipated winning and we figured there would be plenty of time to have good time after the game. Since we played two games back to back at home, there was a little carry over from the week before. Social settings were already arranged, and we picked up where we left off! I reconnected with the group of local girls, and I was on the verge of breaking up with my girlfriend from Huntsville. During that same week, I contacted a girl from Birmingham I met at the back to school block party. As luck would have it, I bumped into her and a few of her homegirls at the liquor store. I had a couple of guys from the team riding with me, so we decided we would hang out with them. It was all coincidental and, after that night, we decided we should hang out again. And, we did—at her place. Nothin' crazy—just having a good time. We had such a good time together, both of us figured we should get together more often. Little did I know we would have a baby girl five years later!

Southern Mississippi came out and played a solid game against us. I didn't rush for more than 100 yards, but I did have over 100 all-purpose yards with no touchdowns. That made two weeks in a row I didn't rush for over 100 yards, or score a touchdown against two unranked opponents. I began to question myself. *Do I have a chance to make it in the NFL?* To be honest, I wasn't sure. I contemplated and analyzed the situation to find a solution to the problem— at that time, I was listed as one of the top five running backs in the country.

But, I wasn't playing like it.

Chapter 13
The Season

The third Saturday in October was traditionally known as the weekend when two powerhouse SEC football teams met—the Alabama Crimson Tide and the Tennessee Volunteers. Media coverage surrounding the game was at a fever pitch, but I wasn't sure why Tennessee got so much publicity. It weren't as if they won a few national titles! Nevertheless, it was a classic match, and it always will be. We were coming off two home victories, but, that week, it was our turn for a road trip to Neyland Stadium which was one of the only schools in the country to seat over one hundred thousand fans. It was my second trip to the stadium, and I remember the band always played "Rocky Top"—a song similar to our "Sweet Home Alabama." Every Tennessee fan knew it, singing it in the stands before, during, and after the game—loudly!

The week of practice leading up to the game we practiced in our indoor facility, and Coach hauled out six-foot speakers, placing them in the corners. Why? He blasted "Rocky Top" so we could get used to the stadium noise! We used silent counts and hand signals to call plays, as well a snap counts. It was a good strategy, and we did the same thing when I played there during my sophomore year, but I didn't realize then the difference it made. But, two years later I was more mature, and I realized we needed to practice the way we were. Unlike my sophomore year, we entered our upcoming game ranked #10 while Tennessee was unranked. If we won, we would be inside the top ten for the first time in the season.

We had a good week of practice as a team, but I worked extra hard that week because I hadn't been in the endzone for the past two weeks. Truth is my games were average—I managed 100 all-purpose yards, but pulled up short of 100 yards for rushing. So, it was my week to show everyone what I could do. Since we played the past two weeks in Tuscaloosa, I allowed myself to be distracted by the off-the-field stuff and, if I didn't step up my game, I realized the ups and downs of our season could easily derail my future plans.

I had to get back on track.

We had a good offensive line coach, and he made the offensive line run extra ten and twenty yards sprints after practice, and I always stayed after so I could run with them. I wanted them to know I was with them at all times, and I believe they respected me for it because I could have been like everyone else, heading to the locker room while they ran.

It was clearly true Tennessee had a talented team led by a phenom quarterback who was starting as a true freshman—Peyton Manning. They featured a good group of running backs, and a solid defense. But, we were who we were—we went to Rocky Top and took care of business even though it was a hard-fought game by two SEC schools sharing a common goal to win a national title. Luckily, we squeaked by with a very close victory, and I felt good about my performance, rushing for over 100 yards and scoring the final touchdown of the game. That touchdown gave us a four point lead, 17-13, leaving Peyton Manning with one last hope only to fall short of victory. As we anticipated, our win put us inside the top ten at#8 with the Ole Miss Rebels staring us in the face. That game wasn't as big as the Rocky Top game, nor was it as big as the game after it. Still, we couldn't overlook it—we had to take the season one game at a time. We stood at 7-0, looking for win number eight and, statistically, I was on point. That was great, but the game with Ole Miss was a test—how badly did I want to make it to the next level? Would I stay focused, building on what I reestablished the previous week against Tennessee?

We had a strong practice week, and things went according to plan. A couple of weeks before, I spent a lot of time with the young lady from Birmingham whom I met at the back-to-school block party. By that time we were seeing each other on a regular basis, yet the more we hung out, the more we realized we were from two completely different backgrounds. Unlike me, she had two parents who were married for more than twenty years, and she didn't attend public high school like I did—for high school, she went to a school of fine arts in Birmingham. We did, however, have something in common—we liked gin and juice. In fact, we began to hang out so frequently, it seemed I was seeing her exclusively. I remained friends with my girlfriends from Huntsville and Montgomery, plus I was in touch with my local female friend after game day in Tuscaloosa. Although I was still a college student, my main focus was trying to make it to the NFL, and I didn't have the time nor energy to develop a serious relationship with anyone—I needed to focus on what I had to do to get to the next level.

That meant getting ready for the Ole Miss game.

Since Mississippi was unranked, the game didn't mean much to them. But, we knew that on any given Saturday, an unranked SEC team could play just as well as a top 10 SEC, or any other team—being at home didn't make any difference, either. We weren't a high performance team, and our reputation was one of playing just a notch above our opponents—the Ole Miss game was no exception.

We started the game sluggishly, and our opponent showed up at our house ready to play. They jumped to a ten point first half lead, and it seemed as if we were in for a long day—our defense couldn't stop them, and our offense couldn't get anything going. It didn't make sense—we had a good week of practice, and we weren't overlooking the team—so, why were we behind by ten points?

The momentum was all Ole Miss until the ghost of Bear Bryant showed up—the rain began to pour, then came thunder and lightning. Game suspended. Both teams returned to the locker rooms for about forty-five minutes until everything blew over and, when the game resumed, we were a different team. We gained ground, but at the half we still hadn't scored any points—however, the second half was a different story, and the energy in our team was palpable!

I began the second half knowing I had to make a touchdown. Our defense stopped their offense with a touchdown that gave us great field position, and we got the ball back inside of Ole Miss territory. We put together a few plays, driving the ball to end with my scoring a TD. It felt good to pull myself out of a slump, but more so for our team to finally get on the scoreboard. After going in at half time trailing 10-0, we took control in the second half to win the game 21-10. I scored a last minute touchdown, sealing the game after our defense caused a turnover. It wound up being a good game for me—100 all-purpose yards with two touchdowns.

****

It was the regular routine after home games—I hooked up with the family, then made my way to the party scene. That game was a little crazy regarding my family because it was the only game of my college career my dad decided to attend with a friend. When he called to request tickets, I couldn't believe he made the effort to see me play.

I should have known better.

After the game, all of my other family members waited to talk to me—but not Eugene Williams. No—before we were out of the stadium, he was gone, and I'm still not sure if he stayed for the entire game. When I exited the locker room, I asked my mother if she had seen him, and she said she did, but I only heard he was there. Oh, well. I confess I was a little disappointed, but I quickly got my head straight—I should have been more surprised if he actually hung around.

During my senior season, I began to feel more confident about making it to the NFL. After the Ole Miss game, I came into my own and, as a team, we were still undefeated with control of our own destiny, leading the SEC West. All we had to do was win. After the comeback win against the Rebels, going into the next week we moved up in the rankings to #6. Headed into week nine we were 8-0, facing another talented, unranked LSU. I wanted to build on the performance from the week before, so during that week of practice I decided I wouldn't talk to anyone on the phone, or visit anyone during the week. We were going on the road to a very hostile environment, and I needed to focus on the task at in front of me if I wanted to give our team a good chance to win. The year before, I suffered an injury that kept me out of the regular season, and it were as if I had a chip on my shoulder. As a sophomore, I scored two touchdowns against LSU and, as a senior, I wanted to top that performance.

Although we were favored to win, we couldn't discount we were on the road against an SEC team, and we knew we would have a fight on our hands. Previously, we experienced issues with handling the ball on kickoffs, so Coach Stallings decided to put me on return kicks. It was a good move for me because it gave me a chance to show the pro scouts what I could do as a return man!

The game turned out as we expected—hard fought. Our defense and special teams made good plays and, early in the game, our offense played well. We clicked, and never fell behind.

I was having a good game returning kicks, rushing, and receiving from the backfield. I scored a touchdown early in the first half, so I was feeling good and only got stronger as the game went on. By the end of the third quarter, we were up 35-10. I scored two touchdowns, rushing for over 100 yards, plus another 100 all-purpose yards. I was #2 in the SEC in rushing, but #1 all purpose, and we went on to beat LSU on their home field, 35-10. It was a statement game for us although, to this point, we hadn't faced a ranked opponent. Still, our team felt good about our chances, and I finally began to feel as if my hard work, focus, and discipline were paying off.

Even though we won the game, we returned home late

and we couldn't party because the LSU game was a night game. By the time we made it back to T-town, everything was closed. That was the time having a girlfriend became very important and, at that time, I wasn't seeing anyone. After a quality win against a good team, I always wanted to celebrate, and it's not fun celebrating alone. I was communicating with a few different girls between games and classes, but I mostly focused on football. There was one girl from Birmingham who interested me and, once we made it back to Tuscaloosa, I called her to see if she were awake—and, if she felt like hanging out with me for a little while. She was, and she did!

Because it was late, most of the clubs were shutting down, and the majority of team members were heading to their girlfriends' places—it was the normal routine for late night away games, win or lose. This was the same young lady I met in the summertime over the gin and juice episode. I knew she liked to drink gin and juice, so on my way to her apartment I stopped off at the package store to pick up Tanqueray gin and orange juice. I recently turned twenty-one and it felt good to walk into the package store, flashing my I.D. when they asked for it.

When I made it to her house it was after two in the morning and, when she answered the door, she didn't look sleepy, at all. In fact, she looked as if she were going on a date! That night when I looked at her, it were as if something came over me—I instantly knew she was the one for me, and by the end of the evening we decided she would be my girlfriend. That was the beginning—dinner. Movies. Companionship.

She was exactly what I needed.

Everything was starting to shape up—I was on my way to the next level in football, and I established a relationship with a nice young lady. Not only that, I was still maintaining a good GPA in school, so eligibility wasn't an issue. All I needed to do was stay focused to make my dream a reality—a chance to play in the NFL.

Our next game was against our first-ranked opponent of the season, as well as a conference game. Mississippi State wasn't traditionally a powerhouse team, but their program was always solid. In their corner, they had a coach who was one of the best in the country, and they always played good ball—but our three previous meetings resulted in wins for the Tide, and I didn't expect this one to be any different. Even so, we didn't let up, and it was back to business as usual.

By then, I was one of the top running backs in the country, and I wanted to build that momentum by making the most of a tough week of practice. The upcoming game wasn't high on the media coverage list, but, as a team, we knew how important it was to give one hundred and ten percent if we wanted to continue toward our goal of winning the National Championship. We entered the game as the #6 team in the country while Mississippi State ranked #20—and, since the game was close, we had the luxury of traveling by bus.

It was a midday game—one of those when, at kick-off it was daylight, but by the end of the game darkness set in. All season we came from behind, and we were a second-half team—it were as if we couldn't get going unless our backs were against the wall. Well, we kicked off first to Mississippi State, and they moved the ball down the field for a touchdown. At this time, their stadium was the smallest in the conference, seating just over 40,000. But, they did this thing with cowbells that would make it sound like over 100,000 fans, and they made it nearly impossible to hear!

When we got the ball back, we drove down the field and scored a field goal. We traded scores in the first half, and went into the half down by five points after I scored a touchdown off a pass from Jay Barker—the score was 14-9. Once again, we were trailing. We weren't down, though—we were so used it that it was just one of those things. We knew what we needed to do, and we got it done. Even though we fell behind by 10 points, 25-15, with less than eight minutes left on the clock, we never felt as if we wouldn't win the game. We scored two late touchdowns to take the game 29-25, and it was a quality win for us. But the next game was the game of the season!

The Iron Bowl.

The Iron Bowl was more important to some people in the state of Alabama than the National Championship game. For us, however, it was the next game on our schedule to get to the National Title game, and Auburn felt the same way. Both teams were undefeated which was uncommon— two SEC teams, late in the season, from the same state. Both were inside the top ten, and we cracked the top five coming in at #4—Auburn was #6. National media hype was in full swing, and it was the game to showcase talent.

It could easily make or break careers.

It was another strong week of practice because we knew were in for a hell of a fight. We drove to Birmingham the night before, and played on our own campus field—for years, Birmingham's Legion Field was the host stadium for both teams' home games for the Iron Bowl. That Iron Bowl in particular was the last one for our Third World Posse, making the game bittersweet.

Ever since my first year with the team, we knew we had the talent in our class to win a National Title although we lost a couple of our key players—some to injury, others to transfers, and those who received a draft bid by the NFL. As a senior, this was my fourth and final Iron Bowl and, even though we had our challenges, we felt good about our chances with the pieces we had in place. The previous year we experienced a 22-14 loss to the Tigers in Jordan-Hare Stadium, so the question was would I finish 2-2, or 3-1 in the game.

We knew we didn't want a repeat of the previous week's game, and we came out firing on all cylinders. I scored the first of our three first-quarter touchdowns to jump to a 21-0 lead in the first half. For the first time in the season, we were off to a good start, and we couldn't have picked a better game to hit our stride early!

The Tigers fought their way back in the game during the second half, and it almost started to feel like what we did to teams earlier in the season—they scored two touchdowns to make it a 21-14 game in the fourth quarter with a chance to tie or go ahead. But we weren't having any of it, and our defense wasn't going to allow that to happen. We ended up winning the game 21-14, and earned a spot to play in the SEC Championship game! In years past, to win such a game so late in the season meant an automatic ticket to play for the National Title—instead, we needed to play in the conference title game. We played in each of the conference championships since it began in 1992 and, each year, we played against Florida and we were 1-1 against them. That year? They were in our way to the National Title.

After winning the Iron Bowl, the fans were ecstatic—and, why wouldn't they be? After all, it meant an entire year of bragging rights! But, our team knew we had to keep our eyes on the prize, and we went into the SEC Championship game with a mindset geared toward getting it done. Ranked #3, if we won we would play for the National Title. Florida was #6, and probably would not play for the title if they won.

The two previous SEC Championship games were played in Birmingham Legion Field, and to play on the Georgia Dome field for the first time was a nice atmosphere. The crowd was loud, and we came out with the first drive of the game and scored a touchdown. We traded scores during the first half until we fell 17-10 at halftime—but, again, it wasn't pressure for us because we were in similar situations several times during the season.

We took a 23-17 lead late in the fourth quarter before they took a 24-23 lead to end the game on a Jay Barker last drive interception. Overall, I felt good about my performance, but it was a bummer we lost—I gained over 100 all-purpose yards, and no touchdowns. Even though I felt the sting of our loss, I still felt I offered a good performance as well as put myself in a good position to be noticed by the NFL scouts. The loss dropped us down to #6 in the polls, taking us out of the national title race.

After the game, most of the team went back to Tuscaloosa, most of the seniors staying in Atlanta. I decided to stay and hang out with family and friends because I loved the city, and any time I had a chance to visit there, I tried my best to make it happen. Honestly, there was a time when a few of my teammates and I visited to party, and things got out of control. There was a huge fight, and I ended up getting stabbed and had to be rushed to the emergency room—fatal if the knife entered one more inch to the left. Luckily, the puncture wound was one inch from my heart, and ended up being only a flesh wound.

But, this trip would be nothing like that one. We had a good time hanging out, and even though we lost the game, we felt good about the way we played, losing by only one point. It still stung because we worked hard all season, and ended without winning the national title—and, with only one loss, we still finished the season ranked inside the top ten at #6. Luckily, our ranking was good enough that we received an invitation to play in the Citrus Bowl, facing the #13 ranked Ohio State Buckeyes.

Getting invited to bowl games was great because it served as one of the big promotions during recruiting. Players definitely wanted to play for a team that would qualify for an invitation to a bowl game and, in of all my previous three years, we played in bowl games. The beauty of playing in a bowl game? Perks. Universities playing in bowl games received millions of dollars, and each player got big gifts from all the sponsors—all of which were against the rules for regular games. Receiving gifts for playing sports in college was illegal, so it allowed schools to give money and gifts to the student athletes. If a team didn't make it to a bowl game, it was a bad season. We received money for travel expenses—more miles, more money.

We played the Citrus Bowl in Orlando, Florida which wasn't far from Prichard. I wished we played in California so I could get a big check, but the Citrus Bowl was fine. It was home to one of the biggest tourist attractions in the United States, Walt Disney World—and, the Orlando Magic had Shaquille O'Neal, so it was a fun place to hang out. I admit it—not having the stress of playing for a national title made the situation a lot more relaxing!

The bad thing about bowl season was it was during holiday break. So, while school was out and all the other students would go home for holiday break, football players had to remain on campus for practice. So bowl season had its pros and cons. In my previous three bowl games we won them all, and I really couldn't see any reason this one would be different. I didn't have a problem staying on campus or in the city, because I felt right at home with my local family. We had a great two weeks of practice and, though the game didn't have any great significance, as a team we always wanted to win.

We didn't prepare differently than we did when we still were in the title hunt, and we had to report a week before the game—one of the advantages of going to a bowl game. Not a bad gig—Orlando was a great place to be in the middle of winter with warm, blue, sunny skies. In previous years, we drove to the bowl games, but that year we decided to fly. Mom was employed at the Mobile Regional Airport at the time, so she was able to use her employee discount to get a decent rate on flights. The amount we paid for our plane tickets was a lot cheaper than the cost of driving, so we bought our tickets and kept the rest in our pockets. We met up in Mobile with the same group of guys I hung out with during the season, and caught our flight.

One thing I should mention—at one of our after-game parties we were hanging out together, and word got back to the coaches that we were partying hard. Yes, I partied, but I was still trying to maintain my focus of making it to the NFL. So, since we had to stay on campus for practice during the Thanksgiving Holidays, we decided to hang out and party a little from the Iron Bowl to the weekend of Thanksgiving. We put together a string of parties and, during those parties, I was using marijuana occasionally. It was a good way to relax and enjoy the holidays away from home. Well, the Monday after we returned to practice, the coach hit us with in-house drug testing. There was a list of players on the suspect list, including myself.

We failed.

From the Iron Bowl to the Thanksgiving Holiday we had some big parties. I didn't make them all, but, those I did attend, I really enjoyed myself, and it was my first time to fail a drug test. The good thing about it was the results wouldn't be back for seven days—after the SEC Championship game. After we took the test, I knew I wouldn't pass, and I just wanted to hear what discipline would be handed down.

We had to report to a meeting after the SEC Championship game—test results were in, and everyone who didn't pass had to stay after the meeting. The coaches revealed the results, and we had to take a second test before the bowl game. If we failed, no bowl game. No gifts. No money. I wasn't concerned about the gifts or money because if I made it to the NFL, I would buy my own gifts with my own money. After the first test I didn't smoke anymore, so I figured the next one would be fine.

We took the second test the week before leaving for Orlando, and we had to take another one when we made it to Orlando. Before all the testing began, I already thought I wouldn't use marijuana after the holidays—I had to focus on making it to the NFL. So, when we met at the airport, everyone was clean and sober. We took an early morning flight to get the best rate as well as to ensure our arriving on time, although we weren't due to check-in and be present for the first team meeting until six o'clock.

Hotel check-in time was at three o'clock, and our flight made it to Orlando around ten-thirty That gave us some time to kill, so we checked out the city—only, we didn't have a ride, so we pitched in for the limo service at the airport. It so happened the guy who was the limo driver was also a pimp. We explained to him who we were, and the reason we were there, and it turned out he had a relative who played in the NFL for a number of years.

Once he knew we weren't law enforcement, he explained to us what he had going on. He made us a few offers, and we decided to take him up on one of them. It was a group of us and only one of him, and some of the guys in our group were pretty big. We ended up going to a house somewhere in the city, and when we got there it was really funny—a nice house without much furniture, and women in different rooms. The women seemed so much older—I was twenty-one, and they were at least thirty. We went in, but I really didn't feel comfortable with the idea. I guess the main thing was I didn't feel as if I were in any danger because I wasn't drinking alcohol, and definitely wasn't using marijuana. Some of the guys had a few drinks, but I decided not to participate in any of the activities—I figured someone had to have a level head in case things turned south. Everything went well, we exchanged info with the driver/pimp, and vowed we would return to see him during our week's stay.

I never did.

CHAPTER 14
THE NFL DRAFT

My final game as a member of the University of Alabama Football Team was in the Florida Citrus Bowl—# 6 University of Alabama Crimson Tide versus #13 Ohio State University. We were in Orlando for an entire week, but it wasn't long enough—we lost. During my entire career at 'Bama, we never lost two games in a row, and we didn't want it to start with that game. But, to be honest, win or lose, the game didn't produce any team reward after losing the SEC Championship—we were out of the race for the title. Ohio State was lower in the polls than Alabama and it was going to be a good game, but the most important thing for me was to know I could prove myself worthy of a chance to play at the next level. That's what it was all about . . .

The NFL.

I led the SEC in all-purpose yards, and ran a tight race for #1 to finish the season with over 1300 yards rushing. Believe me—a back rushing for over a thousand yards in a season against SEC opponents was a big deal! Up until then, Coach Stallings didn't have a running back to rush over a thousand yards in a season, and we had a string of NFL backs to come out prior me. Since I out-performed them, I figured my chance of making it to the NFL was good. In fact, my dream of making it to the NFL motivated me to have a good game. Plus, the Ohio State head coach did a TV interview before the game during which he called me "Sherman Smith." If I had any complacency about the game, I erased it when I heard that and I had an instant chip on my shoulder. Since the interview took place early in the week, I'm not sure if anyone else caught the error in his statement, but, from that point on I promised myself the Ohio State coach would never forget my name again!

Practice week was great, and I felt good about our chances to win. Nonetheless, Ohio State was a good team, and there were a few guys on their team who would go on to be first round picks in the NFL Draft—even a future Heisman Trophy Winner. We knew we had to play a good game to win. I performed well over the course of the season, but I didn't have a super break out game under my belt even though I was second in the SEC in rushing, and first in the all-purpose category. The Florida Citrus Bowl was my last real chance to make a lasting impression.

And, that's exactly what I did.

It was a good back and forth game and, in the first half, I broke a few good runs, plus caught a few passes from the backfield. My rhythm was good, and by halftime I was well over 100 all-purpose yards—a respectable accomplishment since their defense was one of the best in the country. Putting up good numbers against them was impressive—in fact, I was on my way to the biggest game of my college career against a quality opponent!

We struck first, and they came right back to score a

few big special team plays, including a first-half touchdown for me. By halftime, the score was tied at 14-14.

The third quarter started out much the same, and both teams scored fourth quarter field goals for another tie score of 17-17 with a minute left in the game. By the end of the third quarter, I set the record for the most rushing yards in a bowl game for any Alabama running back. Earlier in the season and against Arkansas, I set a school record for the most consecutive carries in a game—fifteen. So, when we were tied at 17-17 with a minute left on the clock, we got the ball back—that's when I set the all-time record for the most all-purpose yards in a bowl game on a game winning touchdown pass. I finished the game with 359 all-purpose yards—a new NCAA Bowl game record! That day, I earned the game MVP Award, and I thought my performance was good enough to impress the scouts. The game was hard fought and well-played by two worthy opponents, and I thought it ironic the best game of my college career was also the last game of my college career.

When the game was over, I had to rush downtown with my Mom and Coach Stallings to receive the MVP trophy at the awards ceremony. Coach Stallings and I spoke before a very excited crowd of mostly 'Bama fans, and the coach from Ohio State spoke after the game, as well. He got my name right, and congratulated us on our victory over his team.

Then, it was done.

The City of Orlando treated us well, and it was time to leave town. I believed the game took me over the edge in the eyes of the NFL scouts, and making it to the NFL was still my main focus.

At that point in my college career, it was customary

for senior players to move out the dorms and off campus, the location to be paid for by coaches or anyone wanting to contribute. My eligibility was no longer in question because I played all four of my seasons, so after the game I decided to return to school to enroll in the classes I needed to graduate. My advisor informed me I needed to complete at least one more semester to graduate with my Bachelor Degree. That bit of news left me with a decision to make— since it was only the first week of the semester, I could withdraw, and set my sights on the NFL, or I could finish college. By the second week of that semester, I received a nice letter from the Bowl Committee, asking me to play in the Senior Bowl game.

The Senior Bowl was played in Mobile since I was a child and I grew up attending the game, always wanting to play in it. It was just as the name implied—a college all-star game comprised of the top seniors in the country. The teams are divided by North and South, much like old Civil War days, and, of course, as a Mobile native and playing for Alabama, I played for the South. Plus, it was convenient, and I didn't have to travel far.

After my performance in the Florida Citrus Bowl, I wasn't sure if there were anything I could do in the Senior Bowl to raise my stock. I had second thoughts about playing in the game, but I finally chose to play for unselfish reasons. The City of Prichard gave me a key to the city, and my high school planned a ceremony at the school. I recalled some of the other guys who played at Blount High and Alabama returned, proud to represent their schools. My high school jersey number was already retired, so they decided on a 'Sherman Williams Day' on January 21st in Prichard. Who could say no to that?

At the time, I still didn't have an agent, and my only

professional advice was from my godbrother in Miami. Most guys had agents advising them regarding playing in the game, and they had to consider whether playing would potentially hurt or help their stock, not to mention missing a week of classes. But, the game was played early in the semester, so missing a week wasn't a big deal.

Even though I enrolled that semester, my mind was still focused on making it to the NFL, but I always had a Plan B. I enrolled with thought if my chances to make the NFL didn't look good, at least I could continue to pursue my college degree with hope of getting a job in my field. I thought if I didn't make it, I could be a good high school football coach.

After the Citrus Bowl, I was officially eligible to sign with an agent without jeopardy of losing eligibility—or the school's being placed on some type of probation. I asked my godbrother to initiate an investigation to scope out my real chances, so he snooped around the NFL circle, reading up on analysts' comments. Coming out of the Citrus Bowl, my name was high on the board, and some projected me as high as the first round. That's why I really didn't want to play in the Senior Bowl, risking injury. I also had to consider since I was no longer playing with 'Bama, my insurance policy was no longer in force.

By that time, I started to exclusively date my girlfriend from Birmingham. I thought by claiming a girlfriend it would cut down some of the drama of dating, and things looked promising. For me, Senior Bowl week was distracting since I was playing and practicing on the same field I played on as a kid. People who didn't see me for many years requested pieces of my time, and I wanted to be respectful to them. As a result, my time was divided, and I needed to retool my focus on the game.

The Senior Bowl was always a big deal in the city and, after my godbrother and I talked about my playing in the game, we also discussed the possibility of my moving to Miami to complete my mission. Moving to Miami meant withdrawing from school, so I decided I would wait until after the Senior Bowl to make such a difficult decision. I wanted to be in an NFL setting with NFL scouts, as well as experience the interviews to figure out how I compared to other players in the game. It was particularly wise for me to play since both teams were coached by NFL coaching staffs.

Overall, it shaped up to be a great experience, and our South squad ended up with the Indianapolis Colts coaching staff under Head Coach, Jim Mora. But, the Senior Bowl was such a big deal for the city of Mobile it came with a level of fanfare, and my being a local didn't make it easier.

I checked out of school, and made my way to the city. Only a few years earlier I thought I would never have a good feeling about coming back to the Mobile/Prichard area, especially after the drama in my high school and early college days. This time, however, I felt as if I rose above the negativity surrounding the city, and it would be a positive experience.

It was.

As soon as I announced I accepted the invitation to participate in the Senior Bowl, the Senior Bowl after-party planning was in full swing. A few of Da Fellas were still living and hanging around the city, waiting to get together for old times' sake, and when I gave them the go ahead, they put everything in motion. I arrived in the city a day or so early, wanting to spend time with my mom at the house in which I grew up. I had always had a room in my mom's house and, whenever I was in the city, I never had to worry about a place to stay. I admit, it was a comfort I enjoyed!

Before the bowl game, I didn't smoke pot or drink, and I promised myself I was going to quit using until after being drafted into the NFL. I stayed true to my word—I accomplished too much to piss it all away. So, I buckled down, and focused. During the time between the Citrus Bowl and the Senior Bowl, I started hitting the weights in an effort to maintain strength as well as prevent injury. That year, we had four or five players from our roster playing in the Senior Bowl, and the Third World Posse was deep.

The things the Senior Bowl committee planned for us was enough to keep the average player busy. For me, it was a lot—the fame and popularity was cool, but some of it went overboard. Let's face it—Mobile isn't a tourist city, and there aren't many attractions. We stayed in what was then the Riverview Adams Mark Hotel, one of the nicest Mobile had to offer. It was pre-911, so security wasn't as beefed up—on one level, we had our game room and meeting area, and meals were served on the same floor. Late night snacks were always available, and everything we needed was at our disposal.

The 'meet and greet' consisted of checking in, receiving itineraries for the week, and breaking off into individual stations to meet with position coaches in order to be ready the next day. The South team practices were held at area high schools in Mobile with the first practices open to the public. Later in the week the practices were private, fast paced, and moving from one station to the next. Coming from a school like 'Bama, I didn't see anything I hadn't already seen while playing for the Crimson Tide.

Time flew. The first night we had a nice party out on the Battleship, one of Mobile's main attractions. It was fun, but my mind was on the bigger picture—I had to get out there, show the coaches my worth, and I couldn't be thinking about partying. That would come later. In fact, I blocked myself from most of the activity in the city, although I did participate in the assembly held in my honor at my old high school.

Toward the middle of the week, we began the interview process. Each NFL team had someone on the grounds to interview each player and we had to take written exams, including the Wonderlic Test. The Wonderlic Test is a standard test to assess aptitude for learning and problem solving in a variety of situations. Most players take the test before the NFL draft, but we had to take it during the Senior Bowl prior to beginning interviews. The testing didn't bother me, because I knew what I had to do to take my career to the next level. I took the exam and breezed through the interview process, learning on the fly, and I couldn't wait until the game to make my mark. When scouts were around, practice was more important than the game because most of them left before we hit the field to play the game. The scouts evaluated us heavily during practice, and the game was mostly for fun and show—odd, but that's the way it was.

I performed well as the starting running back for the South team during practice and the game, catching a couple of passes and rushing for over fifty yards. I found out later I impressed all the coaches who attended our practices— just what I set out to do! However, even though I signed as a free agent, I still didn't have real expectations. I thought I had a great shot at being drafted, but for which position I didn't know. The other crapshoot was draft rounds—I could be drafted in the first, or the last.

It was an interesting time for me because most of the

other guys already signed with agents. At the time of the Senior Bowl, I was probably the only potential first or second round pick who didn't ink a free-agent contract. I heard stories about how many signed with agents, then borrowed money from them—then, when they actually signed their contracts, those agents got all of their money back, plus interest. They bought cars, clothes, and jewelry—things I didn't need. By the time I was a senior, I had three cars on campus at the same time—a Jeep Cherokee, a Cadillac, and a Lexus 400. I also had multiple watches, too many clothes, and over fifty thousand in my bank account. I acquired all of it from money I made throughout the previous off season, as well as and getting monies from various people throughout the season.

I always held the thought if things didn't turn out well with the NFL, I would return to hustling because it was what I knew. Or, I would stay in school to finish my degree to work a nine-to-five job for someone else. Now, I know my thinking was skewed—school should have come first simply because the percentage of people who made the NFL and stayed in it was slim. I admit, thinking of returning to the hustle shouldn't have been part of the consideration, but my background was one of years and years of bad behavior problems. Despite knowing my actions were wrong, that little voice continued to drive me toward the wrong things and making poor decisions.

I realized I had to overcome it.

After the interviews and a little investigation, I felt as if I had a legitimate chance to make it into the NFL draft. During that week, I informed my godbrother I would make my decision about moving to Miami after returning to Tuscaloosa—I had to talk to a few folks. Until then, I played in the Senior Bowl—my final game as a college athlete. I wanted to enjoy the moment without any stress, and Da Fellas planned a nice party at one of the local night clubs. I looked forward to it, but I had a slight conflict—our University of Alabama Lettermens' Banquet was scheduled for the same night. Strange. But, the University sent a jet to pick us up and fly us back to Tuscaloosa in time for the banquet—a great idea, but I preferred to stay in Mobile and attend the after party with family and friends who traveled many miles to watch me play in the Senior Bowl. I still was going to make the sacrifice to go the banquet, but when we were getting ready to board the jet, the pilot realized there weren't enough seats to accommodate everyone. Perfect! I volunteered to stay, and the rest of the guys headed for Tuscaloosa.

When I returned to Tuscaloosa, I received a letter inviting me to participate in the NFL Combine. Yes! To receive such a letter was a confirmation the NFL wanted to fly me in for a serious look. The NFL Combine was in Indianapolis and, when I read the letter, I decided I needed to really concentrate on being ready when the time came for me to perform. I heard about the way it would probably go down, and I had the chance to experience it for myself! I called my godbrother to let him know I was going to withdraw from school, move back down to Miami, and train for the Combine there. But, when I shared the news with the young lady I was dating, she didn't want me to do that—she thought I should finish school. I understood she didn't want me to be free down in Miami without her, so I made an agreement with her that I would fly her down for a weekend during Valentine's Day. A great strategy—she agreed, and I left promising to respond to calls and pages.

Turned out I didn't withdraw from school immediately. I was still on full scholarship, so the University still paid my rent and school tuition. I stayed long enough that I could continue to live in my apartment for the remainder of the semester, and I figured once the Combine was over, I would return to Tuscaloosa for training. Plus, we always had our own semi-combine on campus—we called it Pro Day. Pro Day was when all seniors on the team had a chance to workout for the pro scouts if they considered trying out for and playing in the NFL. It was great because all seniors at every school didn't have a chance to participate in the NFL Combine, so Pro Day was a way for guys to show NFL scouts their skills.

I packed up with three weeks to go until it was time for the Combine. At the time, I was still in tip-top shape because I continued to work out after the season since I planned to play in the Senior Bowl. Plus, I wasn't smoking or drinking. As a result, when I got to Miami, I only needed a little fine tuning. The guys who arrived before me told me the most important thing was to concentrate on the 40-yard dash. When I left high school I was a consistent 4.3, but I weighed only 178 pounds. By the time of the Senior Bowl, I tipped in at 198 pounds—believe me, twenty pounds and four years can make a major difference! But, I figured I was still at least a 4.4—no more than a 4.5.

I hoped!

After arriving in Miami, I met with my trainer, and we began working as soon as I got there—it was straight from the airport to the gym. I told him I had to be ready within a short time frame, and hammered down Sunday through Friday every week, off on Saturday. It didn't leave much time for hooking up with my old crew, but I did manage to spend some time with them after I was there for a few weeks.

My cousin also lived in Miami, so I took advantage of the opportunity to work out with him. We hooked up and hung out, and he knew I was serious about my message and mission—no smoking. No drinking. No hanging out too much. I was there to work toward making it to the next level and, fortunately, they respected and understood my decision because they watched me play the previous season.

I was one of the top football athletes in the country.

Valentine's Day approached, and I made arrangements with my girlfriend to fly her in for the weekend. The only bummer was the real Valentine's Day was during the work week, so we had to plan our celebration for Saturday, February 10th. We had a great time, and on that day, 1994, we made it official—we were a couple. From my athlete perspective, it made sense for me to have a girlfriend to cut down on some of the distractions. All I wanted to do was concentrate on making it to the next level—mainly the 40-yard dash time, as well as bench press. Then, vertical leap, even though there wasn't a viable way for me to increase my vertical jump.

A couple days after my girlfriend left, it was time to make my way to Indianapolis. From Miami to Indy was a big swing in climate and, as soon as I got off the plane, I felt the cold weather, but it didn't faze me. I focused on the big picture because I didn't know what to expect—but it was nothing like I imagined. When I arrived, they checked me in at the hotel, but the actual Combine was held at the Indianapolis Colts home field, the RCA Dome. Man, was it cold! Luckily, I could take the underground shuttle from the hotel to the stadium field!

Once I arrived at the field, they lumped us into a group, then herded us around as if we were cattle. Before we made it to the physical side, we had to endure different tests that checked every inch of our bodies. If I had a bunion on my big toe, they wanted to know how and why.

After that, we proceeded through the meet and greet sessions, each team having a group of representatives present. Then it was the Wonder Lic test, and long interviews with team representatives. I didn't know how much weight the test had in the whole drafting process, but I never heard of anyone being drafted in the first round because of a Wonder Lic test. Or, vice versa.

OF course, there were teams I didn't want to consider, so I purposefully sabotaged my interview with their representatives. The New York Jets, for example—they were a terrible team, plus they played in cold weather. When I was in the interview with their reps, I talked about the time I was in juvenile court with the second degree murder case. Teams I wanted to join never heard one peep about that! All in all, the Combine was a two to three day gig, and it was a long, exhausting process.

I never made it to the third day.

After the interviews and the physical evaluation, on the second day they sent me to visit the cardiologist. Diagnosis—and enlarged heart, and I couldn't participate in any of the exercises at the Combine. This was during the time when a couple of college players collapsed during games after being diagnosed with the same thing, and the NFL took extra precautions. One of the doctors told me I may never play football again.

Before that day, I was a first or second round pick.

I was devastated! There was a good chance I would never play a down in the NFL—no one would want to draft me, and I felt as if I were living a bad dream.

I flew back to Miami, then called my mother, brother,

and girlfriend, delivering the bad news. I ain't gonna lie—I thought my whole life was over. Everything I worked and sacrificed for no longer made a difference.

I felt as low as the ground.

I second guessed my decision to withdraw from school, but, when I got back to Miami, my brother told me I should get a second opinion. It was a good idea, and it made sense to me, so I went back to Alabama to see cardiologists in Mobile and Tuscaloosa. A week later the NFL got in touch, advising me to fly to New York to meet with a different cardiologist. I went, but I never found out the results of those trips. The doctor in Mobile agreed with the Combine doctors, but the Tuscaloosa doctors said there was nothing to be concerned about. After my trip to New York, the NFL contacted me to let me know I could participate in workouts.

My next opportunity would be at Pro Day.

Since Pro Day was in Tuscaloosa, I decided to move back there to train at our facility. Although I was not enrolled in school, I was still on scholarship so I could keep my apartment for the remainder of the semester. The kicker was I didn't know if teams would still be interested in me given the hubbub about the heart issue. Since it could go either way, I still didn't want to lose focus on the big picture of playing in the NFL. Through it all I stayed faithful, believing everything would workout for the best while continuing to workout and train. And, of course, staying away from drugs and alcohol.

My girlfriend was still in Tuscaloosa, so there was no need to be out in the street and, by the time Pro Day rolled around, I was back in top condition. My 40 time was a 4.3, and my weight was good at 198 pounds.

I was ready to play.

Pro Day was a good day for me, but I wasn't sure if I impressed the scouts again. But, after Pro Day, one of the Alabama coaches told me a rep from the Dallas organization asked a lot of questions about me. Had asked about the weed smoking during the bowl game, and I thanked my lucky stars I took the urine test in Indiana during the Combine.

Then it was over.

Not knowing my status was a killer, and I wished I hadn't sabotaged my chances with lesser or cold-weather teams. But, the Cowboys were interested, and I found myself thinking about the time I told my mom I would play for the Dallas Cowboys one day—I was ten. I also told her I would buy a big house and move her into it. In some ways, it was difficult to comprehend my dreams were on the brink of coming true—a few other teams showed interest, but once I knew the Dallas Cowboys were considering me, all other teams came in a distant second.

And, so, I waited.

It was a bittersweet time. I felt powerless—I did everything I could do to make the NFL, and all I could do was wait. Did I regret anything? Probably. The drugs? Alcohol? Maybe not then. I found comfort by hanging out with my girlfriend and members of the Third World Posse who were still in town and, as the draft got to be closer, I took extra care not to smoke or drink, hoping I would become a Dallas Cowboy.

The draft was in NYC that year, and most guys who were 'first round locks' were invited to draft headquarters. I didn't receive an invitation since I was listed as the third or fourth running back to be drafted. That year, the draft class was loaded with quite a few running backs who were potential first rounders. A couple of them did make it in the first round, and the Heisman Trophy winner was a running back that year. In general, the 1995 draft represented the strongest players available.

If I were invited to New York, I'm not sure I would have gone—instead, one of the local car dealerships sponsored me by having a draft party at a hotel. That way, my family and friends could enjoy the draft day experience. You know—people I could trust. Or, so I thought.

Two days before the draft, one of the Dallas scouts contacted my brother, telling him he wanted to attend the party. Well, when I heard that there was no doubt in my mind I was high on the Dallas Cowboy's list. Still, I really didn't know when or where I would be drafted—that year the Cowboys decided to trade away their first round draft pick for later round choices. I was nervous because after the heart condition and failing a prior drug test, I wasn't sure about my stock.

****

Finally! Draft day! The anticipation among my family and friends was on the ceiling, and the moment I wanted throughout my life finally arrived—to be selected to play for an NFL team. Everyone who traveled to Mobile to attend the draft party arrived, including the one scout for the Cowboys. Except my girlfriend—she opted not to attend, but she called throughout the day.

The draft party was held at the hotel, and I decided

to reserve a room on an opposite floor from the party. There were quite a few people at the party, and I stayed with them for the majority of the day. However, we had to provide the draft official a legitimate phone number in case I was drafted, and the team wanted to talk to me.

Folks were drinking and having a good time, and that year four running backs went in the first round. After the Dallas Cowboys traded away their first round pick, I decided to excuse myself and went to the other room I reserved just for myself. I had the draft phone line tied to my room phone.

The first round ended.

After missing the first round, I started to wonder— would a team draft me at all? Halfway through the second round, number forty-six, the Dallas Cowboys had their first pick of the '95 draft.

Sherman Williams.

After I received the news, I returned to the party and, when I entered, everyone clapped and cheered. I'm not sure I can describe how I felt—a very intense feeling came over me. My years of sacrifice paid off.

I was now an official member of the Dallas Cowboys Football Organization.

Chapter 15
Bright Lights

Finally, my life-long dream became a reality—I was poised to be a member of America's Team, the Dallas Cowboys! I have to admit, it was a little overwhelming when I thought about the opportunity in front of me—playing with some of the best players to ever play the sport. All the years playing on the playground, in the backyard, or anywhere else I could find to play football were worth it, and being the forty-sixth pick in the 1995 draft for the Dallas Cowboys made everything official. Being drafted was exciting itself, but to be drafted by the Cowboys? Well, that was icing on the cake!

My draft party was filled wall to wall with family, friends, former teammates, and local businessmen—but the one person who meant more to me than anyone else in this world—Ms. Betty Ruth Williams—was there. My strength, My motivation. My mother. No one was happier for my success because despite everything we endured together, we finally reached the pinnacle. Mom was a soft spoken woman, never over excited about most things, but when it came to football? She was one enthusiastic woman!

She yelled and screamed play after each play, and her being a Dallas Cowboys fan all made it that much sweeter for her.

After the Cowboys traded their first round pick that made me the first selection for the Cowboys in the '95 draft, immediately after their selection the phone rang—it was Jerry Jones! As it turned out, that phone call was the first of many with Jerry, but the first call was probably the biggest thrill because he called to congratulate me, as well as welcome me to the team. We chatted for a few minutes, and he told me he was excited to have me aboard, I thanked him for the opportunity, and our conversation ended with his informing me he would send his private jet to pick up his scout and me first thing the following morning.

It was a whirlwind I never imagined.

I continued to party, but there was one person missing—my girlfriend. She decided she would rather stay in Tuscaloosa, allowing me the space to enjoy the occasion with my family and friends. She felt since we were together for such a short time, it wasn't her place to be there. I tried to convince her to come because I knew after such a monumental evening I would need companionship. If I were drafted, I would need someone to share my celebration—if not, I would need a shoulder to lean on. But, no matter how hard I tried, she maintained her position that it wasn't her place to attend.

The party was packed with a room full of very attractive young women that night, and one of my friends introduced me to a nice girl who was a local Mobile native. We met, talked and, later that night, we became friends. I couldn't stay up to late because I had to be at the airport first thing that morning. The companionship was nice, but my first priority was making sure I was up early the next day, ready to go.

Finally, I was on my way to Dallas.

When I arrived, a member of the media greeted me, which wasn't a surprise. I wasn't nervous, however, because I was already familiar with the media—coming from Alabama, we had plenty of media coverage. After a few minutes with the press, I was on my way to the Cowboys' Headquarters located at One Cowboy Parkway, Irving, Texas—also known as Valley Ranch. A Cowboy veteran greeted me, and I was aware my job was to fill a back-up role. But, in his mind, I could tell he maybe thought I was there to replace him—even so, he seemed to be a nice fellow.

After my brief encounter with him, I was escorted to the main office where I met Jerry Jones. I realized talking to someone over the phone and face to face were two different things—the excitement seemed much more genuine in person. We had a good conversation about goals and expectations, and afterward I attended a scheduled press conference. Throughout my career, I was never big on the media, but I understood the purpose of it. Alabama media coverage was big, but the Dallas Cowboys media coverage was gigantic, and I found I had to grow up fast!

I was drafted on the first day, but it was still happening which was part of the reason Jerry's and my meeting was brief. As I toured the facilities, a few current players were there working out or getting treatment and, on a couple of occasions, I heard them ask about 'The White House.' My first thought was the obvious—where the President of the U.S. lived—so I blew it off, and kept moving. Only later would I learn of their meaning of the 'White House.'

The tour reminded me of a college recruiting trip—meeting players, greeting staff, and being escorted to various locations. It was interesting—before I arrived in

Dallas, I didn't have any expectations, and when I got there I still didn't have any. But after touring the facilities, I knew I was in a good place. The Cowboys won back to back Super Bowls, and the entire atmosphere screamed they were a winning franchise. The chemistry reminded me of my high school days, and it didn't take long to feel comfortable with being a part of the organization.

During the flight home, I reflected on my success—I could finally rest a little. I overcame the obstacles of a young black man born and raised in Prichard, Alabama, and I proved the nay-sayers—those who said I was good, but too small—wrong. Despite any perceived physical shortcomings, I achieved my goal, and I escaped the prison system unlike my friends from Prichard. After all the drugs, sex, guns, and violence I began to think of the money I was about to earn, and the things I would purchase with it. I knew as soon as I landed in Mobile, I needed to contact my brother to ask when he would begin salary negotiations. Some of the guys who drafted before me signed contracts, but, when he called Jerry to begin the talks, they weren't ready to discuss it.

After we heard that, we decided to put together a marketing campaign to obtain endorsements, and I met with trading card dealers. I started earning money by signing trading cards, and I also filmed a cereal commercial. Some of my trading card deals required me to be on site, and before I knew the business side of things, one of the card companies requested my appearance in Los Angeles for a photo shoot that would pay me $5,000. However, our first rookie mini camp was scheduled on that same day. My brother—also my agent—didn't know the business side and, after we talked, we decided since I hadn't signed a contract with Dallas I should take advantage of the opportunity to make some money.

All the first picks for every team in the 1995 NFL Draft were there. It was surreal—I thought the lights in Dallas were bright, but, when I got to L.A., I saw lights brighter than daylight! When I stepped off the plane it were as if I stepped in to a different country, and I realize it's a city that's constantly in the spotlight, especially since we were only a year out from the O.J. Simpson national trial.

When I got to the shoot for the card dealers, an authentic Dallas Cowboys uniform with #20 on the back and front were waiting for me. Helmet, too. From the second I arrived, it was clear the photo shoot was arranged by professional, large, brand name companies. One in particular had a good line-up of events to take place over that weekend, plus a meet and greet with several brand name corporate sponsors. I was looking forward to hanging out with all the other guys who were first picks for their teams, but once I left the field at L.A. Coliseum and made it back to the locker room, I checked my pager and my brother was trying to reach me.

When I contacted him, he informed me the Cowboys were trying to reach me because they wanted me there for mini-camp—and, he already had my flight scheduled to leave LAX. As much as I wanted to stay in L.A., I knew I had to get back to Dallas. It was a tough situation because I had come too far to give it up like that—still, I had a commitment to the card dealers. They were a little reluctant at first to give me the money we agreed on to make the appearance, but after we talked they decided to give me the five grand. Since most of the other first picks already signed contracts with their teams, they understood their obligations, and it boiled down to multi-million dollar contracts verses a $5000 photo shoot. Some made the photo shoots, some didn't. So, I had a choice to make—contract or photo shoot.

I chose the contract.

At the time, Barry Switzer was Head Coach of the Dallas Cowboys. He realized I wasn't in camp, and he called my brother looking for me. When he told them where I was and what I was doing, he was furious. He was cussing and fussing for me to get my butt to Dallas on the first thing out of L.A.!

I made it to Dallas on the second day of a three day mini camp. Coach Switzer and I talked, and he let me know what he expected from me as well as the rest of the team. I felt good because I was finally starting to get paid for playing the sport that I truly loved.

The mini camp was the first chance I had to meet everyone who was drafted in '95, or brought in as a rookie free agent. When we arrived, we moved immediately into a two-bedroom apartment, and my roommate was a guy who drafted in a later round. The organization felt both of us were a little under weight, and they put us on a rigorous training program. It worked out because we got along well, and we could support each other as we integrated into the team. At the time, I was only 5'8" and 195 pounds, but the staff wanted me to play at around 205 pounds, so I had to add on ten pounds of muscle. But, I didn't want to compromise my speed by the extra weight—so, the organization assigned a retired former Cowboys player to work with us during our summer workout sessions. By the time mini-camp rolled around, both of us were in good shape. However, because my roommate was a defensive player, once the coaches called practice to order, he and I didn't see each other—even during the first rookie mini-camp.

During that summer in Dallas, I learned my way quickly because I hooked up with some local guys, and started hanging out in the clubs—drinking and smoking again. The night life scene in Dallas was totally different than Prichard or Tuscaloosa—whenever I hung out in the clubs with the local guys, they introduced me as the first pick for the Dallas Cowboys. That announcement always drew attention to myself and the guys with us, and that's how I was introduced to the city. That meant late nights, and bright lights—I had yet to learn when the bright light shone directly on me, I was blinded to true colors of my environment.

Things began to move fast for me in the city. I thought on the field would be a big adjustment, but the rookie mini-camp was pretty simple. The only pieces of equipment we had were helmets and sweat pants. We didn't practice in equipment, and at this stage of the game we were one hundred percent professional—no need for all the extra stuff. If we needed to be taught the fundamentals, we wouldn't be on that level. However, the lack of equipment didn't hamper our competitive drive—we were there to do our jobs, equipment or not.

We had a great group of guys drafted that year, plus free agents who became impact players, and some of us clicked instantly. I became good friends with a couple of guys who ended up making the practice squad in addition to my roommate and another defensive player. We hooked up after practice, and hung out in the city. In Dallas, a Dallas Cowboy always had things his way—when we hung out in the clubs we went in a group because it was safer, and if we needed or wanted anything, all we had to do was ask.

I was having the time of my life!

Even though I picked up some of my old habits, I was still training hard, not taking anything for granted. During the summer when mini-camps were over, most players headed to their home state until the next mini camp. When training camp wasn't in session, I ran with some local guys, smoking and drinking, and sometimes I felt as if I were hustling again. Keep in mind, they weren't average, working-class guys—I knew early on they were holding large bills. Nonetheless, football was still my top priority, and being on the Dallas Cowboys team was a dream come true. I couldn't do anything to jeopardize my opportunity to play on the team. You know the phrase 'birds of a feather flock together?' Well, I heard it all my life, but looking back on it, I began to realize the truth in that statement. Before being drafted, the only thing I thought about was the Dallas Cowboys, never considering the city in general. One of my favorite clubs was The Iguana Mirage, known as one of the hottest clubs in the city.

More bright, blinding lights.

There was another guy who was new to the city—who was already a big name in the industry, and he came to the Cowboys as a free agent. He and I were pitched together to do media events for the local stations, and we became good friends. Each Friday, he threw parties at a local club, and my roommate and I always attended. Doing so was how I introduced myself to Dallas, and I began to feel as if I really made it. I was hanging out with a famous player, and I was part of the back-to-back Super Bowl Champion Dallas Cowboys organization—I was on top of the world!

Our next mini camp included the entire team, veterans and rookies, and it was then I met everyone. By then, I was semi-acclimated to the city—knew my way around certain parts. One day after veterans camp, a teammate and I had an appearance at Reunion Arena—the Dallas Mavericks home court—but I didn't have my car from college, nor had

I signed a contract with Dallas. So, I hopped in to ride with him, and before we made it to the Reunion, he said he needed to make a stop. I had no clue where we were going until we pulled up to the Men's Club. When we walked in, fifteen or so veteran players greeted us—big name players. It was the first time I had the opportunity to hang out with my teammates at one of the upscale strip clubs in the city. We were certainly in good company—politicians, prominent business owners, pro athletes, doctors, lawyers—big guns from everywhere. Suit and tie required. But, because I was with someone famous, we were allowed to enter as we were—casual. He sat down to talk to the rest of the fellas, and I sat down, ordering myself a drink. I felt I had made it, so I could start living a little. Camps were going well, training was working, and I felt good.

While in the club, a few of the veteran players offered to treat me to a strip tease. I declined the offers, and used my own money to get dances—I wanted them to know I wasn't new to the strip club scene, and I guess they were surprised I wasn't star struck. Coming from 'Bama, playing on national TV every week, I thought I was a rock star like them. I hadn't yet signed a contract, but I still had a good sum of cash saved in my college account. I carried my own weight, and they didn't need to show me the ropes. I did, however, hear one of the guys ask a player if he were going to make it by the White House. I recognized the name from my initial visit to Dallas, but, I ignored it—I figured since they weren't asking me, it was none if my business.

Finally, we headed to the event and, afterward, we headed back to my car which was parked at Valley Ranch. When dropping me off, he told me to follow him. From being there the entire summer through mini camps, I somewhat knew my way around, but not enough to know exactly where I was going. I followed anyway, and I didn't have to drive very far—we never left Valley Ranch. We pulled up to a nice gated community—he in his black-on-black Mercedes S550, and me in my black Lexus, pulling up to the gate like gangsters. He tapped in the code, and I swung around to enter through the gate. Then he took the lead again—we turned a few curves, and made it to the back of a nice subdivision. When we pulled up to the residence it was like an exotic car show, limousines included. It was a nice neighborhood—one to which I wasn't accustomed.

The White House.

Chapter 16
A Changing Tide

Dreams are funny. You can dream about something for your entire life and, when it finally comes true, you realize it's as good—or, better—than you thought it would be. Turns out it was worth the time you spent dreaming—most of it, anyway.

That's the way it was for me—I dreamed of being a high school football star. A college football star. A Dallas Cowboy. I worked my butt off, and I played hard—I felt as if nothing could bring me down. Nothing could make me fall.

But, fall I did.

The tide changed, and I found myself mired in a mess I never imagined. For the first time in my life I was surrounded by lies. Deceit. Video tapes.

And, prison.

If only it were a dream . . .

A Note from the Author

Living the life I lived—winning a championship ring on every level of football, then being incarcerated to serve a fifteen-year sentence on a drug conspiracy charge—compelled me to write this book. I thought such a book would not only highlight the many obstacles young men face on a daily basis in the urban communities across the U.S., but with the hope some child faced with similar circumstances will not make the bad decisions I made along the way. Hopefully, someone will read my story and be influenced to make a life-changing decision. Maybe some teacher in a classroom of kids will—through these pages—see the warning signs, recognizing a certain student may be on the verge of traveling my tragic path. I want to be as honest and forthcoming as possible without being vulgar or disrespectful.

I stole. I lied. I worked hard. I shook hands with the President of the United States, and I sold drugs on the streets. I scored the first touchdown in a national title game, and I served time in Federal prison. I fathered two kids in high school. I have experienced two of life's greatest extremes—the highest of the highs, and the lowest of the lows. And, along my way, I learned experience is the best teacher.

I hope someone across the world can use my experience written in this book to learn something. This is the first book of a three-volume series that will walk you through the transformation of a boy to a man. *Crimson Cowboy* will depict the life of a boy who was gifted with a skill and talent that teams pay millions for, only to squander it all because he could not escape the temptations of the peers he associated with for the greater part of his life. This book details the rise of a state champ, national champ, and Super Bowl winning drug dealer.

Book Two tells the story of how a guy was locked up for fourteen years in Federal prison where he was able to reconnect with our Heavenly Father.

Book Three speaks of a man who is totally transformed by his own life's decisions—a strict vegetarian who doesn't use drugs or alcohol while leading a life pleasing to God while becoming the president of a 501(C3) nonprofit organization—the Palmer Williams Group. An organization formed from behind the walls only to be lived out on the outside.

Thank you to all my readers who support me on these projects.

LAUNCHING IN NOVEMBER, 2015!

PEACE BETWEEN THE LINES

by

Sherman Williams

Continue to follow Sherman's story as he lives life as a Dallas Cowboy, then falls into the chasm of the Federal prison system.

PROFESSIONAL ACKNOWLEDGMENTS

CHRYSALIS PUBLISHING AUTHOR SERVICES
Editor—L.A. O'Neil
chrysalispub@gmail.com

JEN KRAMP STUDIOS
Cover Art
jenkramp@gmail.com